Communications
in Computer and Information Science   2108

Rationale

The CCIS series is devoted to the publication of proceedings of computer science conferences. Its aim is to efficiently disseminate original research results in informatics in printed and electronic form. While the focus is on publication of peer-reviewed full papers presenting mature work, inclusion of reviewed short papers reporting on work in progress is welcome, too. Besides globally relevant meetings with internationally representative program committees guaranteeing a strict peer-reviewing and paper selection process, conferences run by societies or of high regional or national relevance are also considered for publication.

Topics

The topical scope of CCIS spans the entire spectrum of informatics ranging from foundational topics in the theory of computing to information and communications science and technology and a broad variety of interdisciplinary application fields.

Information for Volume Editors and Authors

Publication in CCIS is free of charge. No royalties are paid, however, we offer registered conference participants temporary free access to the online version of the conference proceedings on SpringerLink (http://link.springer.com) by means of an http referrer from the conference website and/or a number of complimentary printed copies, as specified in the official acceptance email of the event.

CCIS proceedings can be published in time for distribution at conferences or as postproceedings, and delivered in the form of printed books and/or electronically as USBs and/or e-content licenses for accessing proceedings at SpringerLink. Furthermore, CCIS proceedings are included in the CCIS electronic book series hosted in the SpringerLink digital library at http://link.springer.com/bookseries/7899. Conferences publishing in CCIS are allowed to use Online Conference Service (OCS) for managing the whole proceedings lifecycle (from submission and reviewing to preparing for publication) free of charge.

Publication process

The language of publication is exclusively English. Authors publishing in CCIS have to sign the Springer CCIS copyright transfer form, however, they are free to use their material published in CCIS for substantially changed, more elaborate subsequent publications elsewhere. For the preparation of the camera-ready papers/files, authors have to strictly adhere to the Springer CCIS Authors' Instructions and are strongly encouraged to use the CCIS LaTeX style files or templates.

Abstracting/Indexing

CCIS is abstracted/indexed in DBLP, Google Scholar, EI-Compendex, Mathematical Reviews, SCImago, Scopus. CCIS volumes are also submitted for the inclusion in ISI Proceedings.

How to start

To start the evaluation of your proposal for inclusion in the CCIS series, please send an e-mail to ccis@springer.com.

Jaime A. Riascos Salas · Vinícius Rosa Cota ·
Hernán Villota · Daniel Betancur Vasquez
Editors

Computational Neuroscience

4th Latin American Workshop, LAWCN 2023
Envigado, Colombia, November 28–30, 2023
Revised Selected Papers

 Springer

Editors
Jaime A. Riascos Salas (ID)
Institución Universitaria de Envigado
Envigado, Colombia

Vinícius Rosa Cota (ID)
Istituto Italiano di Tecnologia
Genoa, Italy

Hernán Villota (ID)
Institución Universitaria de Envigado
Envigado, Colombia

Daniel Betancur Vasquez (ID)
Institución Universitaria de Envigado
Envigado, Colombia

ISSN 1865-0929   ISSN 1865-0937 (electronic)
Communications in Computer and Information Science
ISBN 978-3-031-63847-3   ISBN 978-3-031-63848-0 (eBook)
https://doi.org/10.1007/978-3-031-63848-0

This Springer imprint is published by the registered company Springer Nature Switzerland AG
The registered company address is: Gewerbestrasse 11, 6330 Cham, Switzerland

If disposing of this product, please recycle the paper.

Preface

The human brain, with its unparalleled complexity, remains one of the most enigmatic and challenging research frontiers. To address this challenge, the Latin American Workshop on Computational Neuroscience (LAWCN) creates a multidisciplinary community of scientists and professionals, to disseminate cutting-edge discoveries and methodologies around computational neuroscience, artificial intelligence, neuroengineering, and neuroscience. This series of events, initiated in 2012 at the Federal University of Rio Grande do Sul (UFRGS), and formally established in 2017, has consistently promoted collaborative knowledge-building through its biennial conferences, held in vibrant Brazilian cities like Porto Alegre (2017), São João del-Rei (2019), and São Luís de Maranhão (2021).

The IV LAWCN (https://lawcn.co/) was held between 28–30 November 2023 in Envigado (Antioquia - Colombia), marking a significant expansion of the conference's reach beyond its Brazilian origins. Envigado, located within the metropolitan area of Medellín, provides a culturally rich and dynamic setting. Notably, Envigado is recognized as a UNESCO Global Network of Learning City, underscoring its commitment to knowledge exchange and advancement, aligning with the core objectives of LAWCN. This edition of the event was the result of a strategic collaboration between the University Institution of Envigado (IUE), led by the Faculty of Engineering and its research group "Grupo de Investigación Tecnologías Emergentes Sostenibles e Inteligentes-GITESI", and the Colegio Colombiano de Neurociencias (COLNE). This organizational effort underscores the inter-institutional commitment to advancing computational neuroscience research in Colombia and the Latin American region. Furthermore, the continued support from the International Brain Research Organization (IBRO) enabled both travel grants, promoting accessibility for international researchers, and a focused roundtable addressing the current challenges of gender diversity in neuroscience.

The IV LAWCN successfully fostered a stimulating intellectual environment for knowledge exchange, network building, and research collaboration, reaching up to 250 attendees who engaged in the dissemination of findings through the oral presentation of 28 research papers and 15 posters. The conference featured nine distinguished keynote speakers from France, the USA, Norway, Brazil, and Colombia, ensuring a rich international perspective. Additionally, it offered valuable insights from the Federation of Latin American and Caribbean Neuroscience Associations (FALAN), a unique roundtable on gender diversity, the launch of the Brain-Computer Interface LATAM community, and a short course in computational modeling using NetPyNE.

All manuscripts submitted to the Workshop were subjected to a rigorous single-blind peer review process, by a minimum of three experts from our Program Committee (PC). The papers within this volume are distinguished by their originality and methodological strength in areas such as artificial intelligence, machine learning, computational neuroscience, and brain-computer interfaces. We offer our profound gratitude to the strategic partners (listed below), keynote speakers, authors, reviewers, and all participants. Your dedication and expertise were instrumental in facilitating this exceptional conference and the resulting publication, which serves as a valuable resource in the ongoing quest to unravel the complexities of the brain. Thank you!

May 2024   Jaime A. Riascos Salas
                                            Vinícius Rosa Cota
                                            Hernán Villota
                                            Daniel Betancur Vasquez

Organization

Editor

Jaime A. Riascos Salas   Institución Universitaria de Envigado (IUE), Colombia

Co-editors

Vinícius Rosa Cota   Istituto Italiano di Tecnologia, Italy
Hernán Villota   Institución Universitaria de Envigado (IUE), Colombia
Daniel Betancur Vasquez   Institución Universitaria de Envigado (IUE), Colombia

Organized By

Institución Universitaria de Envigado (IUE), Colombia
Colegio Colombiano de Neurociencias (COLNE), Colombia
Pontificia Universidad Javeriana de Cali (PUJ), Colombia
Universidad del Valle (UniValle), Colombia

Conference Chairs

Jaime A. Riascos Salas (Chair)   Institución Universitaria de Envigado (IUE), Colombia
Lina Vanessa Becerra Hernández (Co-chair)   Colegio Colombiano de Neurociencias (COLNE)/Pontificia Universidad Javeriana de Cali (PUJ)/Universidad del Valle (UniValle), Colombia

Organizing Committee

Daniel Betancourt Vasquez   Institución Universitaria de Envigado (IUE), Colombia
Dante Augusto Couto Barone   Federal University of Rio Grande do Sul (UFRGS), Brazil

Edwin Alexander Moncada Acevedo	Institución Universitaria de Envigado (IUE), Colombia
Efraín Buriticá Ramírez	Universidad del Valle (COLNE), Colombia
Hernán Villota	Institución Universitaria de Envigado (IUE), Colombia
Jaime Andres Riascos Salas	Institución Universitaria de Envigado (IUE), Colombia
Jonier Rendón	Institución Universitaria de Envigado (IUE), Colombia
Lina Vanessa Becerra Hernández	Universidad del Valle/Pontificia Universidad Javeriana de Cali/COLNE, Colombia
Maria Marta Molinas Cabrera	Norwegian University of Science and Technology (NTNU), Norway
Silvia Vanegas	Institución Universitaria de Envigado (IUE), Colombia
Vinícius Rosa Cota	Istituto Italiano di Tecnologia, Italy

Program Committee Chair

Jaime Andres Riascos Salas	Institución Universitaria de Envigado (IUE), Colombia

Program Committee

Alan Talevi	National University of La Plata, Argentina
Alexandre Surget	IBraiN, Inserm, University of Tours, France
Antônio Roque	University of São Paulo (USP), Brazil
Antonio Fernando Lavareda Jacob Junior	State University of Maranhão (UEMA), Brazil
Betsy Mary Estrada Perea	Institución Universitaria de Envigado (IUE), Colombia
Carlos Dias Maciel	University of São Paulo (USP), Brazil
Carolina Bellera	National University of La Plata, Argentina
Catalina Alvarado Rojas	Pontificia Universidad Javeriana (PUJ), Colombia
Cesar Alberto Collazos	Universidad del Cauca, Colombia
Daniel Betancur Vasquez	Institución Universitaria de Envigado (IUE), Colombia
Daniel Medeiros	Karolinska Institutet, Sweden
Dante Augusto Couto Barone	Federal University of Rio Grande do Sul (UFRGS), Brazil

Diana Francisca Adamatti	Universidade Federal do Rio Grande (FURG), Brazil
Diana Marcela Parra Urrea	Institución Universitaria de Envigado (IUE), Colombia
Diego Alejandro Herrera Jaramillo	Institución Universitaria de Envigado (IUE), Colombia
Edison Pignaton de Freitas	Federal University of Rio Grande do Sul (UFRGS), Brazil
Eduardo López-Larraz	Bitbrain, Spain
Erivelton Geraldo Nepomuceno	Maynooth University, Ireland
Fabien Lotte	Inria Centre, University of Bordeaux, France
Fábio Manoel França Lobato	Federal University of Western Pará, Brazil
Fernando da Silva Borges	Federal University of ABC (UFABC), Brazil
Fernando Marmolejo-Ramos	University of South Australia, Australia
Gabriel Mindlin	Universidad de Buenos Aires, Argentina
Gabriela Castellano	University of Campinas (Unicamp), Brazil
Gustavo Villegas	University of Antioquia, Colombia
Héctor Julián Tejada Herrera	Federal University of Sergipe (UFS), Brazil
Hernán Villota	Institución Universitaria de Envigado (IUE), Colombia
Jaime Andres Riascos Salas	Institución Universitaria de Envigado (IUE), Colombia
Jean Faber	Federal University of São Paulo (UNIFESP), Brazil
Jim Tørresen	University of Oslo, Norway
John Fredy Ochoa	University of Antioquia, Colombia
Jorge Andrés Dapena Ossa	Institución Universitaria de Envigado (IUE), Colombia
Jorge Parraga-Alava	Universidad Técnica de Manabi, Ecuador
Jose A. Salazar	Universidad del Cauca, Colombia
Jose L. Contreras-Vidal	NSF IUCRC BRAIN Center, USA
Jose M. Azorín	University of Elche, Spain
José C. Príncipe	University of Florida, USA
Jose Bernal	DZNE, Germany
Jose Donoso	Ruhr University Bochum, Germany
Julián Mauricio Granados Morales	Institución Universitaria de Envigado (IUE), Colombia
Lilian Konicar	Medical University of Vienna, Austria
Lina Vanessa Becerra Hernández	Universidad del Valle/Pontificia Universidad Javeriana de Cali/COLNE, Colombia
Marangelie Criado-Marrero	University of Florida, USA
María Daniela Concha Vélez	Instituto Tecnológico Metropolitano (ITM), Colombia

Maria Marta Molinas Cabrera	Norwegian University of Science and Technology (NTNU), Norway
Marianna Semprini	Istituto Italiano di Tecnologia, Italy
Mauricio Rangel-Gomez	NIMH, USA
Michela Chiappalone	Universitá degli Studi di Genova, Italy
Nivaldo Antônio Portela de Vasconcelos	Federal University of Pernambuco (UFPE), Brazil
Norberto Garcia-Cairasco	University of São Paulo (USP), Brazil
Omar Andrés Carmona Cortés	Federal Institute of Maranhão (IFMA), Brazil
Oscar Alberto Henao Gallo	Universidad Tecnológica de Pereira (UTP), Colombia
Pablo Alexander Reyes Gavilán	Pontificia Universidad Javeriana (PUJ), Colombia
Patricio Orio	Universidad de Valparaíso, Chile
Paula Marcela Herrera Gómez	Universidad Tecnológica de Pereira (UTP), Colombia
Paulo Rogério de Almeida Ribeiro	Federal University of Maranhão (UFMA), Brazil
Ricardo Erazo-Toscano	Seattle Children's, USA
Rodrigo Alejandro Sierra Ordoñez	University of Szeged, Hungary
Rodrigo Pena	Florida Atlantic University, USA
Salvador Dura-Bernal	SUNY Downstate, USA
Sen Cheng	Ruhr University Bochum, Germany
Vinícius Rosa Cota	Istituto Italiano di Tecnologia, Italy
Wimar Moreno	Instituto Tecnológico Metropolitano (ITM), Colombia

Keynote Speakers

Alexandre Surget	IBraiN, Inserm, University of Tours, France
Catalina Alvarado Rojas	Pontificia Universidad Javeriana (PUJ), Colombia
Fabien Lotte	Inria Centre, University of Bordeaux, France
Jose L. Contreras-Vidal	NSF IUCRC BRAIN Center, USA
Marangelie Criado-Marrero	University of Florida, USA
Maria Marta Molinas Cabrera	Norwegian University of Science and Technology (NTNU), Norway
Norberto Garcia-Cairasco	University of São Paulo (USP), Brazil
Paula Marcela Herrera Gómez	Universidad Tecnológica de Pereira (UTP), Colombia
Salvador Dura-Bernal	SUNY Downstate, USA

Roundtable

Catalina Alvarado Rojas	Pontificia Universidad Javeriana (PUJ), Colombia
Lina Vanessa Becerra Hernández	Universidad del Valle/Pontificia Universidad Javeriana de Cali/COLNE, Colombia
Marangelie Criado-Marrero	University of Florida, USA
Maria Marta Molinas Cabrera	Norwegian University of Science and Technology (NTNU), Norway
Paula Marcela Herrera Gómez	Universidad Tecnológica de Pereira (UTP), Colombia
Yadira Ibargüen-Vargas	University of Orléans, France

Sponsors

Strategic Partners

UNIVERSIDAD
DE ANTIOQUIA

Universidad Cooperativa
de Colombia

UNIVERSIDAD
EIA
Ser, Saber y Servir

UNIREMINGTON®
CORPORACIÓN UNIVERSITARIA
RES. 2661 MEN JUNIO 21 DE 1996

UNIVERSIDAD DE
SAN BUENAVENTURA
MEDELLÍN

UNIVERSIDAD CES
Un compromiso con la excelencia

UF | UNIVERSITY of FLORIDA

université
de TOURS

Université
d'ORLÉANS

Inserm
La science pour la santé _____
_____ From science to health

Contents

Artificial Intelligence and Machine Learning

EEG-Based Classification of Passive Pedaling Speeds Using SVM:
A Promising Approach for Enhancing Lower Limb Rehabilitation
Technologies 3
  Cristian Felipe Blanco-Diaz, Cristian David Guerrero-Mendez,
  Aura Ximena Gonzalez-Cely, Andrés Felipe Ruiz-Olaya,
  Denis Delisle-Rodriguez, Teodiano Bastos-Filho,
  and Sebastián Jaramillo-Isaza

Data Augmentation by Adaptative Targeted Zoom for MRI Brain Tumor
Segmentation 14
  José Armando Hernández

Riemannian ElectroCardioGraphic Signal Classification 25
  Aurélien Appriou and Fabien Lotte

Computational Neuroscience

Evaluation of Wnt/β-Catenin Pathway Modulation on CA3-CA1 Synaptic
Plasticity Model: An Aproximation to Alzheimer Disease 43
  Hernán Villota and Karla Avilez

In Silico Application of the Epsilon-Greedy Algorithm for Frequency
Optimization of Electrical Neurostimulation for Hypersynchronous
Disorders 57
  Gabriel da Silva Lima, Vinícius Rosa Cota, and Wallace Moreira Bessa

Fuzzy Control with Central Pattern Generators for the Locomotion
of Quadruped Robotic Systems 69
  Edgar-Mario Rico-Mesa and Jesús-Antonio Hernández-Riveros

Brain-Computer Interfaces

Comparison of Visual and Kinesthetic Motor Imagery for Upper Limb
Activity 95
  Martha-Rocio Torres-Narváez, Oliver Müller,
  and Alvaro David Orjuela-Canon

Effect of an Imagery Training on Biomechanical Aspects of a Sport Skill
in Gymnasts of the Met Chia Club 106
   Lina María Estefanía Guzmán Riaño, Erica Mabel Mancera Soto,
   and Gustavo Adolfo Pineda Ortiz

Influence of Delays in Functional Connectivity to Distinguish Motor
Imagery Tasks 118
   Pedro Felipe Giarusso de Vazquez, Carlos Alberto Stefano Filho,
   and Gabriela Castellano

Impact of Ocular Artifact Removal on EEG-Based Color Classification
for Locked-In Syndrome BCI Communication 128
   Paal S. Urdahl, Vegard Omsland, Sandra Løkken, Mari Dokken,
   Andres Soler, and Marta Molinas

Author Index 145

Artificial Intelligence and Machine Learning

EEG-Based Classification of Passive Pedaling Speeds Using SVM: A Promising Approach for Enhancing Lower Limb Rehabilitation Technologies

Cristian Felipe Blanco-Diaz[1](✉)(iD), Cristian David Guerrero-Mendez[1](iD),
Aura Ximena Gonzalez-Cely[1](iD), Andrés Felipe Ruiz-Olaya[2](iD),
Denis Delisle-Rodriguez[3](iD), Teodiano Bastos-Filho[1](iD),
and Sebastián Jaramillo-Isaza[4](iD)

[1] Postgraduate Program in Electrical Engineering, Federal University of Espírito
Santo (UFES), Vitória, Brazil
cblanco88@uan.edu.co
[2] Faculty of Mechanical, Electronics and Biomedical Engineering, Antonio Nariño
University, Bogotá D.C., Colombia
[3] Edmond and Lily Safra International Institute of Neurosciences, Macaíba, Brazil
[4] School of Medicine and Health Sciences, Universidad del Rosario,
Bogotá, Colombia

Abstract. Motorized Mini Exercise Bikes (MMEBs), have found applications in Brain Computer Interfaces (BCIs) for rehabilitation, aiming to enhance neural plasticity and restore limb movements. However, processing electroencephalography (EEG) data in this context presents challenges, often relying on discrete on/off control strategies. Such limitations can impact rehabilitation progress and Human-Machine Interaction (HMI). This study introduces a Support Vector Machine (SVM)-based approach to classify passive pedaling tasks at varying speeds using EEG signals. The research protocol involved four healthy volunteers performing passive pedaling induced by a MMEB at two speeds: 30 and 60 rpm. SVM achieved an average ACC of 0.77, a false positive rate of 0.26, and AUC of 0.80, demonstrating the feasibility of accurately identifying passive pedaling at both low and high speeds using EEG signals. These results hold promising implications for improving the design of more robust and adaptive controllers in BCI systems integrated with MMEBs, particularly within the context of lower limb rehabilitation. This research supports the way for enhanced brain-machine interaction, offering potential benefits to individuals with disabilities by facilitating more precise control of rehabilitation devices and advancing the field of neuroengineering. Further exploration of real-world applications and broader implications is necessary to fully harness the potential of this SVM-based approach.

Keywords: Brain Computer Interfaces (BCIs) · Passive Pedaling ·
Speeds Classification · Lower-limb rehabilitation · Motorized
Mini-Exercise Bike (MMEB)

J. A. Riascos Salas et al. (Eds.): LAWCN 2023, CCIS 2108, pp. 3–13, 2024.
https://doi.org/10.1007/978-3-031-63848-0_1

1   Introduction

Brain Computer Interfaces (BCIs) have gained widespread recognition due to their role in bridging human communication with the external environment, facilitated by the extraction and interpretation of brain-related data [2]. These versatile technologies have found application in the control of various rehabilitation devices, including prostheses [16], exoskeletons [4], and Motorized Mini-Exercise Bikes (MMEBs) [9,18]. Notably, Electroencephalography (EEG) stands out as the preferred neuroimaging technique for BCI design, thanks to its non-invasive nature and portability [1]. Nonetheless, the utility of EEG signals is challenged by both physiological and non-physiological artifacts [1,16].

The development of therapeutic interventions utilizing BCIs, particularly those based on MMEBs, has shown promise in generating purposeful pedaling while individuals engage in cognitive tasks. This approach aims to induce cortical rhythms within regions of the brain affected by neurological disorders, such as post-stroke rehabilitation [9]. For instance, Romero et al. introduced a BCI relying on Motor Imagery (MI) pedaling tasks for on/off control of a MMEB, with a focus on post-stroke rehabilitation [18]. However, the exclusive reliance on mental tasks may pose limitations, as some individuals with neuromotor impairments may struggle to imagine movements they are physically incapable of performing, potentially diminishing human-machine interaction and motivation [3,11].

In light of these considerations, several studies have delved into EEG signal analysis during the execution of passive movement tasks facilitated by robotic devices. For example, Nojima et al. reported the potential of training BCI systems with sensory feedback from exoskeletons or electrical stimulation to induce neuromotor recovery in stroke patients [14]. Similarly, Cantillo-Negrete et al. explored the use of a hand orthosis and Intracortical Brain-Computer Interfaces (iBCI) for kinesthetic feedback in MI tasks, showcasing the positive effects of passive assistance on cortical rhythms and accuracy rates [8]. However, while substantial literature has focused on upper limb restoration, knowledge regarding lower limb applications remains limited.

In the system proposed by Romero et al., passive assistance was introduced as sensory feedback to test subjects following pedaling MI tasks [18]. Cardoso et al. extended this system to investigate differences in cortical activity during passive pedaling and pedaling MI tasks [9]. Notably, these studies concentrated solely on passive pedaling at a constant speed, potentially impeding the rehabilitation progress of individuals with disabilities [16]. Consequently, there is a gap in research exploring brain wave dynamics during passive pedaling tasks with varying characteristics, such as speed. For instance, Wu et al. employed EEG to classify attention tasks during treadmill use at different speeds but did not address pedaling tasks [19].

To address this research gap and facilitate the development of more personalized rehabilitation device control strategies based on EEG data, this study presents a machine learning-based methodology for the classification of passive pedaling tasks at varying speeds. A protocol was designed that involves the use of an Motorized MiniExercise Bike (MMEB) to facilitate passive pedaling at two different speeds (high and low) while simultaneously recording EEG measurements. The primary contribution of this paper is the development of a methodology that employs features derived from covariance matrices of EEG signals in conjunction with Support Vector Machine (SVM) for classification of passive pedaling speeds. This approach holds the potential to inform the design of personalized robotic BCI controllers with a specific focus on progressive lower limb rehabilitation.

The paper is structured as follows: Sect. 1 provides an introduction, presenting the state of the art and the contributions of this work. Section 2 details the materials and methods employed in the study. Section 3 presents the results, followed by a discussion in Sect. 4, and concluding remarks and future directions in Sect. 5.

2   Material and Methods

2.1   Motorized Mini Exercise Bike

A Motorized Mini Exercise Bike (MMEB) is a motor-assisted pedal exercise machine designed to facilitate resistance pedaling exercises. It offers assistance in lower limb tasks, making it suitable for passive pedaling when individuals are physically unable to perform active pedaling. In this study, we utilized the MMEB depicted in Fig. 1, which was adapted from previous research with a focus on speed control [9, 18]. Specifically, we configured the MMEB to operate at two distinct speeds: 30 rpm (referred to as low speed) and 60 rpm (referred to as high speed).

2.2   Participants

To ensure statistically meaningful results, participant selection was based on a power analysis conducted using Gpower software [10]. We employed a Gpower with an effect size (Cohen's d) of 2.13, a significance level (α) of 0.05, and a power level of 0.90, guided by previous studies [7, 13]. The analysis indicated that a minimum of four subjects was required. Accordingly, four healthy volunteers were recruited, aged between 25 and 32 years, comprising two males and two females. This study was conducted in full compliance with the Declaration of Helsinki and adhered to the ethical guidelines set by the Ethics Committee of the Federal University of Espirito Santo (UFES/Brazil) under protocol number CAAE:39410614.6.0000.5060.

2.3   EEG Recording

Throughout the experimental protocol, EEG data acquisition was conducted using the OpenBCI board in conjunction with Openvibe free-source software. This setup allowed for precise synchronization of cues with the activation of the MMEB. Electrode placement followed the international 10–20 system, with a focus on electrodes, where lower limb movements have been frequently observed: FC_1, FC_2, C_3, C_Z, C_4, CP_1, CP_2, and P_Z (see Fig. 2) due to the same configuration implementation in similar studies as well as the significant Event Related Desynchronization/ Synchronization (ERD/ERS) results focused around Cz performing passive pedaling as feedback in closed-loop that was mentioned in the literature [5, 7, 9, 18]. Additionally, reference electrodes were positioned at the ear lobes (A1 and A2). EEG signals were sampled at a rate of 250 Hz, and a notch filter was applied to minimize power line interference.

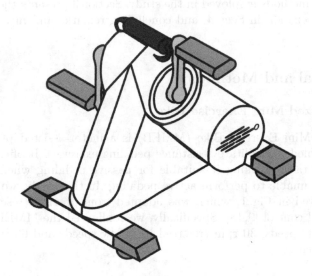

Fig. 1. Schematic of the MMEB used to generate passive pedaling at different speeds.

2.4   Experimental Procedure

The experiment was conducted in a noise-controlled environment to mitigate external artifacts affecting EEG signals. The protocol encompassed the following steps:

1. Participants rested their feet on the MMEB for 1 min without engaging in any mental tasks (baseline).
2. The MMEB was activated within a randomized time frame of 7 to 10 s, operating at either 30 rpm (low speed) or 60 rpm (high speed).
3. After active pedaling, the MMEB was deactivated for an equivalent period to allow participants to rest.

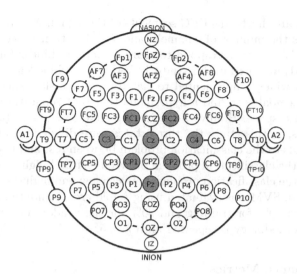

Fig. 2. Spatial distribution of electrodes using the international 10–20 system for EEG.

4. This procedure was repeated 20 times for each speed, resulting in a total of 40 trials per session.
5. A one-minute break was provided between sessions to alleviate mental and physical fatigue. Subsequently, a second session, replicating steps 1–4, was carried out.

2.5 EEG Preprocessing

After generating the EEG database, each EEG signal was segmented into three states: rest, passive pedaling at low speed, and passive pedaling at high speed. Subsequently, each time segment was windowed for 1 s with a 50% overlap, following established conventions [18]. A Common Average Reference (CAR) filter was applied to each segment to eliminate common noise sources. Additionally, a 4th-order bandpass Butterworth filter was implemented, with a frequency range of 1 to 30 Hz, aligning with the spectral characteristics of EEG signals during lower limb movements [5,7].

2.6 Covariance Matrices and Classification

One of the most used features in the literature corresponds to the covariance matrices [15], which are calculated as follows:

$$C_i = \frac{1}{t-1} X_i X_i^T, \tag{1}$$

where C are the covariance matrices, i is the actual sample, t is the number of time samples, X_i is every trial, for $n = 1...N$ where N is the number of trials, where the trials are short-time EEG segments of the signal, $X \in R^{c \times t}$ is the trial considering c as the number of channels, and T is the transposed matrix. Subsequently, these features correspond to classifier inputs. Linear Support Vector Machine (LSVM) was used in this study. LSVM is a machine learning technique, which has been widely implemented to classify motor tasks using EEG signals [2,12], where the goal is to find a hyperplane that best separates two classes of data in a feature space. However, considering that SVM faces binary classification problems, in this study the three states were divided into three groups: **CP1** corresponds to the classification problem between rest and low speed, **CP2** corresponds to the classification problem between rest and high speed, and **CP3** corresponds to the classification problem between low and high speeds. To generalize the method, SVM was evaluated using k-fold cross-validation. The dataset was divided into 70% for training and 30% for the random evaluation. Subsequently, this methodology is repeated until $k = 5$.

2.7   Performance Metrics

To evaluate the SVM performance, the classification Accuracy (ACC), and False Positive Rate (FPR) were calculated. These metrics were defined by Eqs. 2 and 3.

$$ACC = \frac{TP + TN}{TP + TN + FP + FN}, \tag{2}$$

$$FPR = \frac{FP}{TN + FP}, \tag{3}$$

where TP, TN, FP, and FN correspond to the true positives, true negatives, false positives, and false negatives, respectively. It should be noted that the best performance of the SVM is obtained when the ACC is close to 1, while the FPR is close to 0. On the other hand, the Area Under Curve (AUC) provides important information about the rate between the True Positive Rate (TPR) and FPR [7].

3   Results

Initially, ERD/ERS were computed by using a power analysis for two different speeds (speeds 1 and 2) to assess the spatial distribution of spectral behavior during pedaling tasks. To address this, the power spectrum during the passive pedaling was calculated and subtracted from power during rest tasks, as has been done in previous studies [9]. Figure 3 illustrates the ERD/ERS results for an individual, focusing on five specific frequency bands: Delta (1–4 Hz), Theta (4–8 Hz), Mu (8–13 Hz), Low-Beta (13–20 Hz), and High-Beta (20–30 Hz).

The performance metrics are summarized in Fig. 4. Figure 4a displays the ACC for each test subject across the three classification problems (CP1, CP2, and CP3). Among the participants, the lowest performance was observed in S03, with ACC values approximately at 0.79, 0.67, and 0.57 for CP1, CP2, and CP3,

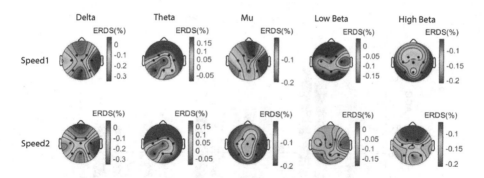

Fig. 3. Spatial distribution of ERD/ERS in the different frequency bands for an individual. Speed 1 and 2 correspond to low and high speeds, respectively.

respectively. In contrast, S04 demonstrated the highest performance, achieving ACC values of 0.93, 0.89, and 0.93 for CP1, CP2, and CP3, respectively. On average, the ACCs were 0.88 ± 0.06 for CP1, 0.81 ± 0.10 for CP2, and 0.62 ± 0.03 for CP3.

Regarding the FPR, S03 exhibited the poorest performance, with FPRs of approximately 0.36, 0.45, and 0.37 for CP1, CP2, and CP3, respectively. In contrast, S01 achieved the best FPR results, with values of 0.15, 0.19, and 0.24 for CP1, CP2, and CP3, respectively. On average, FPRs were approximately 0.20 ± 0.11 for CP1, 0.28 ± 0.13 for CP2, and 0.31 ± 0.06 for CP3.

In summary, the average performance of the SVM in classifying passive pedaling tasks using EEG signals yielded an ACC of approximately 0.77 ± 0.14 and a FPR of 0.27 ± 0.06. In this context, the AUC was calculated and presented in Fig. 5, where it is possible to highlight an average performance close to 0.80. These results surpass chance probability, indicating that the classifier's performance is notably above random chance. These findings suggest the classifier's potential adequacy for practical applications in BCIs for passive pedaling tasks.

4 Discussion

This study introduced a novel methodology for the identification of passive pedaling tasks at different speeds using EEG signals. The approach relied on covariance matrices of EEG signals in combination with SVM classifiers. Despite SVM's initial design for binary classification tasks, we adopted a one-to-one strategy, dividing the classification problems into three distinct groups [12].

The results of this study obtained mean ACC values of approximately 0.88, 0.81, and 0.62 for discriminating between rest and passive pedaling with low speed, rest and passive pedaling with high speed, and passive pedaling with low speed versus high speed, respectively. On average, an overall ACC of 0.77 was obtained. Notably, the highest classification performance was achieved when distinguishing passive pedaling at low speed from rest. This result aligns with

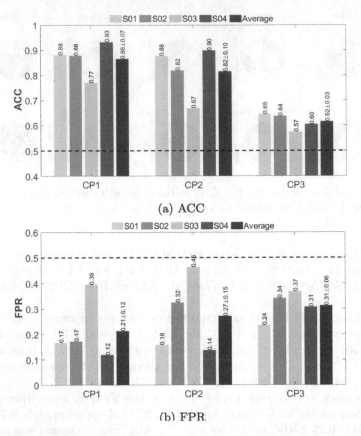

(a) ACC

(b) FPR.

Fig. 4. SVM performance metrics for classifying passive pedaling tasks at different speeds using EEG signals. The practical level of chance computed for the classifier is of 0.5, which is shown as a dotted line.

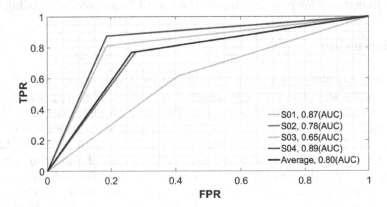

Fig. 5. AUC of the ROC curve for the SVM for detecting passive pedaling at different speeds.

findings in the literature; for instance, Wu *et al.* observed that EEG signal classification during slower-paced walking was more successful compared to faster walking speeds, possibly due to motion artifacts and signal noise associated with rapid position changes [19]. The methodology implemented in this study demonstrated the feasibility of classifying passive pedaling tasks at two distinct speeds, with ACC values consistently above chance.

While the approach of this study to classifying passive pedaling tasks at different speeds is novel, meaningful comparisons can be drawn with existing studies. For example, Romero *et al.* employed covariance matrices and Riemannian geometry to classify MI pedaling tasks after passive assistance, achieving ACC values exceeding 0.90 [18]. However, their approach was limited to MI tasks and constant-speed pedaling, potentially restricting its applicability in progressive rehabilitation scenarios. In another study, Blanco-Diaz *et al.* reported an ACC rate of approximately 0.73 and AUC close to 0.74 for classifying active pedaling using EEG [7]. In other proposals, feature extraction methods related to spatial filtering as Common Spatial Patterns, have been also used to classify pedaling action and rest from EEG signals, reaching an ACC rate of 0.81 [6]. However, in the aforementioned approaches, the pedaling velocity was overlooked. Additionally, nonlinear techniques have been applied to classify passive assistance at different speeds; for instance, Quiles *et al.* achieved an ACC rate of 0.68 in differentiating speed using EEG for a lower-limb exoskeleton, although this approach has not been explored extensively for pedaling tasks [17]. In light of these comparisons, the results reported here fall within an appropriate range, with an average ACC of approximately 0.77 (maximum 0.81), FPR of 0.27 (minimum 0.19), and AUC of 0.80 (maximum 0.89).

The significance of this study lies in the development of a robust and accurate methodology for classifying passive pedaling tasks at varying speeds using EEG signals. Given the importance of passive assistance or sensory feedback in rehabilitation processes [3, 14], our methodology offers promise for the design of more personalized robotic device controllers. These controllers, when integrated into MMEB-based BCI, could enhance progressive rehabilitation strategies significantly.

Moving forward, future research directions should explore algorithmic enhancements and the integration of these strategies into the design of more resilient control systems for MMEB-based BCIs, particularly in the context of progressive rehabilitation. Additionally, addressing potential challenges and limitations, such as motion artifacts and noise in EEG signals during dynamic tasks, will be critical for further improving the methodology's applicability in real-world scenarios.

5 Conclusion

The results of this research demonstrate the feasibility and potential of the methodology based on SVM classifiers and covariance matrices for the classification of passive pedaling tasks generated by a MMEB at different speeds using EEG signals. The study achieved mean ACC values approaching 0.88 for distinguishing passive pedaling from rest, with ACC values of 0.62 for classifying passive pedaling tasks at low and high speeds. Overall, the SVM classifier exhibited an ACC of 0.77, FPR of 0.27, and AUC of 0.80.

These findings carry significant implications for future research and practical applications. Specifically, they open the door for the integration of the developed algorithms into an MMEB speed controller that leverages brain information through a BCI for lower limb rehabilitation. As researchers move forward, further exploration and refinement of these methodologies offer the potential to enhance the control of rehabilitation devices and contribute to the progressive rehabilitation of individuals with neuromotor impairments.

Finally, this research underscores the transformative potential of BCIs within the field of rehabilitation technology. It holds the promise of improving mobility and enhancing the quality of life for individuals facing neuromotor challenges. It is the aspiration of this research that it will inspire continued exploration and innovation in this vital area of healthcare technology.

Acknowledgments. The authors would like to thank the Federal University of Espírito Santo (UFES/ Brazil) for the support to this research, Coordination for the Improvement of Higher Education Personnel (CAPES) (001), and Espirito Santo Research Support Foundation (FAPES)/I2CA (Resolution N° 285/2021). The authors would also like to thank those who participated in this study.

References

1. Abiri, R., Borhani, S., Sellers, E.W., Jiang, Y., Zhao, X.: A comprehensive review of EEG-based brain-computer interface paradigms. J. Neural Eng. **16**(1), 011001 (2019). https://doi.org/10.1088/1741-2552/aaf12e
2. Aggarwal, S., Chugh, N.: Signal processing techniques for motor imagery brain computer interface: a review. Array **1**, 100003 (2019). https://doi.org/10.1016/j.array.2019.100003
3. Amo Usanos, C., Boquete, L., de Santiago, L., Barea Navarro, R., Cavaliere, C.: Induced gamma-band activity during actual and imaginary movements: EEG analysis. Sensors **20**(6), 1545 (2020). https://doi.org/10.3390/s20061545
4. Biao, L., Youwei, L., Xiaoming, X., Haoyi, W., Longhan, X.: Design and control of a flexible exoskeleton to generate a natural full gait for lower-limb rehabilitation. J. Mech. Robot. **15**(1) (2022). https://doi.org/10.1115/1.4054248
5. Blanco-Díaz, C.F., Guerrero-Mendez, C.D., Delisle-Rodriguez, D., de Souza, A.F., Badue, C., Bastos-Filho, T.F.: Lower-limb kinematic reconstruction during pedaling tasks from EEG signals using unscented kalman filter. Comput. Methods Biomech. Biomed. Eng. 1–11 (2023). https://doi.org/10.1080/10255842.2023.2207705
6. Blanco-Díaz, C.F., et al.: Evaluation of temporal, spatial and spectral filtering in CSP-based methods for decoding pedaling-based motor tasks using EEG signals. Biomed. Phys. Eng. Exp. (2024). https://doi.org/10.1088/2057-1976/ad2e35

7. Blanco-Díaz, C., Guerrero-Mendez, C., Bastos-Filho, T., Ruiz-Olaya, A., Jaramillo-Isaza, S.: Detection of pedaling tasks through EEG using extreme learning machine for lower-limb rehabilitation brain-computer interfaces. In: 2023 IEEE Colombian Conference on Applications of Computational Intelligence (ColCACI), pp. 1–5 (2023). https://doi.org/10.1109/ColCACI59285.2023.10225911
8. Cantillo-Negrete, J., Carino-Escobar, R.I., Carrillo-Mora, P., Barraza-Madrigal, J.A., Arias-Carrión, O.: Robotic orthosis compared to virtual hand for brain-computer interface feedback. Biocybern. Biomed. Eng. **39**(2), 263–272 (2019). https://doi.org/10.1016/j.bbe.2018.12.002
9. Cardoso, V.F., et al.: Effect of a brain-computer interface based on pedaling motor imagery on cortical excitability and connectivity. Sensors **21**(6), 2020 (2021). https://doi.org/10.3390/s21062020
10. Faul, F., Erdfelder, E., Lang, A.G., Buchner, A.: G* power 3: a flexible statistical power analysis program for the social, behavioral, and biomedical sciences. Behav. Res. Methods **39**(2), 175–191 (2007). https://doi.org/10.3758/BF03193146
11. Flusberg, S.J., Boroditsky, L.: Are things that are hard to physically move also hard to imagine moving? Psychon. Bull. Rev. **18**, 158–164 (2011). https://doi.org/10.3758/s13423-010-0024-2
12. Guler, I., Ubeyli, E.D.: Multiclass support vector machines for EEG-signals classification. IEEE Trans. Inf. Technol. Biomed. **11**(2), 117–126 (2007). https://doi.org/10.1109/TITB.2006.879600
13. Hosseini, S.M., Shalchyan, V.: State-based decoding of continuous hand movements using EEG signals. IEEE Access (2023). https://doi.org/10.1109/ACCESS.2023.3270803
14. Nojima, I., Sugata, H., Takeuchi, H., Mima, T.: Brain-computer interface training based on brain activity can induce motor recovery in patients with stroke: a meta-analysis. Neurorehabil. Neural Repair **36**(2), 83–96 (2022). https://doi.org/10.1177/15459683211062895
15. Omari, S., Omari, A., Abderrahim, M.: Multiple tangent space projection for motor imagery EEG classification. Appl. Intell. 1–9 (2023). https://doi.org/10.1007/s10489-023-04551-2
16. Padfield, N., Zabalza, J., Zhao, H., Masero, V., Ren, J.: EEG-based brain-computer interfaces using motor-imagery: techniques and challenges. Sensors **19**(6) (2019). https://doi.org/10.3390/s19061423
17. Quiles, V., Ferrero, L., Iáñez, E., Ortiz, M., Cano, J.M., Azorín, J.M.: Detecting the speed change intention from EEG signals: from the offline and pseudo-online analysis to an online closed-loop validation. Appl. Sci. **12**(1), 415 (2022). https://doi.org/10.3390/app12010415
18. Romero-Laiseca, M.A., et al.: A low-cost lower-limb brain-machine interface triggered by pedaling motor imagery for post-stroke patients rehabilitation. IEEE Trans. Neural Syst. Rehabil. Eng. **28**(4), 988–996 (2020). https://doi.org/10.1109/TNSRE.2020.2974056
19. Wu, C., Qiu, S., Xing, J., He, H.: A CNN-based compare network for classification of ssveps in human walking. In: 2020 42nd Annual International Conference of the IEEE Engineering in Medicine & Biology Society (EMBC), pp. 2986–2990 (2020). https://doi.org/10.1109/EMBC44109.2020.9176649

Data Augmentation by Adaptative Targeted Zoom for MRI Brain Tumor Segmentation

José Armando Hernández(⊠)

Université Paris-Saclay, ENS Paris-Saclay, CNRS, Centre Borelli,
91190 Gif-sur-Yvette, France
jose-armando.hernandez-gonzalez@universite-paris-saclay.fr

Abstract. This study presents a novel data augmentation methodology to enhance the scientific outcomes achieved during the Brats 2023 challenge. The 3D-UNet neural network, initially proposed by Ronneberger et al. in 2015 for biomedical image segmentation, is described. Its performance is evaluated in the segmentation of human brain tumors utilizing authentic MRI data from the BraTS 2023 challenge. The specifics of the data augmentation algorithm and its importance in the context of MRI images of this nature, as well as the utilized network architecture, are briefly expounded. Finally, future directions are outlined.

1 Introduction

The emergence of Data-Centric machine learning has recently garnered attention as a means to enhance model performance. Deep learning models, such as Convolutional Neural Networks (CNNs), are prone to overfitting. This study hones in on the challenges posed by data augmentation techniques, particularly in the realm of image classification and segmentation. These techniques are pivotal in enabling deep learning models to mitigate overfitting and deliver improved performance. This is especially pertinent in the context of MRI medical images, where limited sample sizes due to regulatory constraints and data privacy concerns present significant hurdles in effectively training neural networks.

To achieve improved robustness on new data, there are several data augmentation techniques proposed, such as flipping, rotation, scaling, brightness adjustment, and elastic deformation, augmenting data for semantic segmentation based on the random image cropping and patching (RICAP) method, generally compared affected the learning process when training a 3D U-Net standard [1].

The BraTS 2023 competition is the top reference for segmentation algorithms, and one of its challenging tasks is the development of new data augmentation techniques. Previous editions of BraTS, the results of which are mentioned in the MICCAI conference, show significant advances in this field of artificial intelligence. In this sense, the automatic segmentation of tumors through machine learning represents a promising alternative solution to this growing problem for

J. A. Riascos Salas et al. (Eds.): LAWCN 2023, CCIS 2108, pp. 14–24, 2024.
https://doi.org/10.1007/978-3-031-63848-0_2

timely and efficient diagnosis. Center Borelli is particularly interested in creating medical applications in an agile way.

Considering the above, this paper studies a new recursive data augmentation method for segmenting human brain tumors with the 3D-UNet network within the framework of the BraTS challenge to achieve advanced segmentation models in iterative development cycles. 3D-Unet is chosen because it is a widely studied architecture with a good response, and its complexity is adequate as a reference for benchmarking.

The document is organized as follows. First, a brief review of state-of-the-art 3D-UNet for biomedical image segmentation along with a brief explanation of the characteristics of acquired BraTS Dataset [2,3] MRI images in Sect. 2. The 3D-UNet architecture is briefly described in Sect. 3. The process of data preparation, training, and validation of the network with the proposed data augmentation algorithm is described in Sect. 4. The results and metrics obtained are discussed. Finally, Sect. 5 concludes the paper and presents ideas for future work.

2   The T1, T1ce, FLAIR and T2 Types of MRI Images

The MRI images labeled as T1 and T2 correspond to image sequences acquired using different parameters to highlight different anatomical or pathological features in the brain. In MRI terminology, using different parameters in the acquisition is referred to as different *weightings*.

Let us define some important time metrics used in MRI.

Tissue can be characterized by two different relaxation times - T1 and T2 [4]. T1 (longitudinal relaxation time) is the time constant determining the rate at which excited protons return to equilibrium, i.e., realign with the external magnetic field. T2 (transverse relaxation time) is the time constant which determines the rate at which excited protons reach Equilibrium or going out of phase with each other, i.e., to be disordered concerning the external field.

Time to Echo (TE) is the time between the RF pulse's delivery and the echo signal's receipt. Repetition Time (TR) is the time between successive pulse sequences applied to the same slice.

T1-weighted images are obtained using a long TR and a TE. These images provide good soft tissue differentiation, allowing for clear visualization of anatomical structures in the brain, such as the cerebral cortex, basal ganglia, and focal lesions. Normal brain tissues appear in these images with a bright signal, while fluids and lesions appear dark.

T2-weighted images are obtained using a short TR and a long TE. These images highlight pathological changes in the brain, such as inflammation, ischemia, and demyelinating lesions. Fluids, such as cerebrospinal fluid (CSF), appear bright in these images, while soft tissue and lesions may appear darker.

FLAIR (Fluid-Attenuated Inversion Recovery) is a particular sequence of T2-weighted images that suppresses the cerebrospinal fluid (CSF) signal, allowing better visualization of brain lesions and periventricular pathologies. This

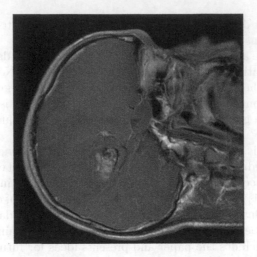

Fig. 1. Example of a T1 MRI brain image. It shows the tumor region in a light gray color compared to the darker brain tissue.

sequence is beneficial for detecting demyelinating lesions and areas of gliosis, as well as for assessing lesion burden in diseases such as multiple sclerosis.

See Fig. 1 for a typical T1 MRI image with a tumor lesion. Table 1 shows the characteristics of different tissues from scanned MRI image types.

Table 1. Comparison of Tissue Representation in MRI Weighted Images. The image presents a brightness gradation depending on the particular brain tissue [4].

Tissue	T1 Weighted	T2 Weighted	FLAIR
CSF (Cerebrospinal Fluid)	Dark	Bright	Dark
White Matter	Light	Dark Gray	Dark Gray
Cortex	Gray	Dark Gray	Dark Gray
Fat	Bright	Light	Light Gray
Inflammation	Dark	Bright	Bright

The MRI images Fig. 7 provided by the BraTS competition have the structure of four channels labeled as follows.

Annotations (Labels):

- Label 0: Unlabeled Volume (black color)
- Label 1: Necrotic and non-enhancing tumor core (NCR/NET) (dark green color)
- Label 2: Peritumoral edema (ED) (yellow color)
- Label 3: GD-enhancing tumor (ET) (green color)

3   Method

According to [5] the performance of different architectures GaNDLF [6] including U-Net concerning the Dice loss function for application of brain extraction is expected to be 0.97 ± 0.01 with U-Net, ResUNet 0.98 ± 0.01, and FCN (Fully Convolutional Network) 0.97 ± 0.01. For brain tumor sub-region segmentation U-Net 0.65 ± 0.05, ResUNet 0.71 ± 0.05, FCN 0.62 ± 0.05, and UInc 0.64 ± 0.05.

Other works have made an approach to medical images using a zoom strategy [7], but it has not been used from the point of view of data augmentation to improve results. The objective is to present a new data augmentation methodology that allows for improving several of the current metrics of the 3DUnet network used for the competition and, simultaneously, using this developed model as part of the algorithm. The dataset is BraTS 2023 Glioma, and the neural network architecture is 3D-Unet; see Fig. 4.

The BraTS 2023 dataset [3,8,9] contains 1200 MRI images of the brain describing a 3D volume of $240 \times 240 \times 155$ pixels and four channels (wt1, FLAIR. Tice, Wt2 as described in the previous section).

Computationally, the neural network will have more difficulties in reaching its optimal configuration depending on the number of parameters of the network, which is why it is ideal to have a network of an adequate size in the number of pixels that adapts to the problem at hand. That is the principle of the proposed algorithm in a self-adaptation approach zoom and learn, or ZOLE [10]. In the case of brain tumor segmentation, the available training images are large and, at the same time, sparse for CNN models. For example, in most cases, the tumor does not cover more than 10% of the image. In that case, a network that processes $240 \times 240 \times 155$ pixels is not optimal. And so we choose to reduce the size to $128 \times 128 \times 128$ without losing the context [11] and having to train a network of 5,645,828 parameters.Figure 3.

Hence, given the diverse shapes tumors may exhibit, the primary objective is to pre-train a model capable of initially discerning the coordinates of the center of mass of interest. Subsequently, this model generates a new zoomed [10], scaled, and rotated image (refer to Fig. 2) with a focus on tumor anatomy rather than brain anatomy. Importantly, this process maintains contextual information crucial for tumor mass localization.

If the size of the tumor requires it to adaptively, a new scaling of the $64 \times 64 \times 64$ image can be given with the consequent reduction of parameters for training (Fig. 5).

Figure 6 describes the architecture trained with the BraTS2023 dataset, specifying the different layers and their interaction at the code level.

Figure 7 describes the four channels T1CE, FLAIR, T2, and the three-color mask representing each class.

18   J. A. Hernández

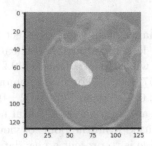

Fig. 2. Data augmentation Adaptative by rotation zooming on the target tumor image
$128 \times 128 \times 128$ pixels

Algorithm 1. Data Augmentation Algorithm

1: **function** ADAPTATIVE_ZOOMIG_TRANSFORM(I: input image, M : mask)
2:      $XYZ \leftarrow$ center_of_mass_coordinates
3:      $NewImage \& Newmask \leftarrow$ zooming_new_targeted_image
4:      $Q \leftarrow$ [Rotation, H_flip, V_flip]   ▷ list of available transformations
5:      **for** _ $\leftarrow 1$ **to** len(Q) **do**
6:          $T \leftarrow$ random choice from Q
7:          **if** $T =$ Rotation **then**
8:              $\alpha \leftarrow$ random integer between 15 and 75
9:              $I_t \leftarrow$ rotate(I, α)
10:             $M_t \leftarrow$ rotate(M, α)
11:         **else**
12:             $I_t = T(I)$
13:             $M_t = T(M)$
14:         **end if**
15:         $Q = Q - T$ ▷ remove T from set Q
16:     **end for**
17:     **return** I_t, M_t
18: **end function**

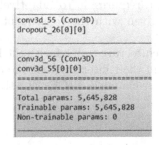

Fig. 3. number of 3dunet training parameters image $128 \times 128 \times 128$ pixels

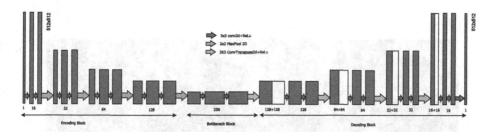

Fig. 4. The U-Net architecture is characterized by its U-shaped structure, consisting of a contraction section (encoder) and an expansion section (decoder). Here, we should see the U shape with its Encoding, Decoding Blocks, and Bridging (Bottleneck) blocks.

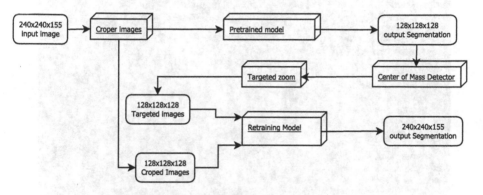

Fig. 5. The figure describes the entire Data augmentation Targeted Zooming process.

4   Results

As described, this new method requires iteratively creating the new dataset in a data-model driven approach, which is why there is no test bed like the one that exists in Evaluating Augmentations for BraTS, which benchmarks against that uses a fixed model architecture GaNDLF [6] model, and measures optimization achieved in DiceScore from the augmentation data.

$$\text{DICE} = \frac{2 \times |X \cap Y|}{|X| + |Y|}$$

Where:

- DICE represents the Dice coefficient used as a loss function in image segmentation tasks.
- $|X \cap Y|$ denotes the cardinality of the intersection between sets X and Y.
- $|X|$ represents the cardinality of set X.
- $|Y|$ represents the cardinality of set Y.

```
s = inputs

#Contraction path
c1 = Conv3D(16, (3, 3, 3), activation='relu', padding='same')(s)
c1 = Dropout(0.1)(c1)
c1 = Conv3D(16, (3, 3, 3), activation='relu', padding='same')(c1)
p1 = MaxPooling3D((2, 2, 2))(c1)

c2 = Conv3D(32, (3, 3, 3), activation='relu', padding='same')(p1)
c2 = Dropout(0.1)(c2)
c2 = Conv3D(32, (3, 3, 3), activation='relu', padding='same')(c2)
p2 = MaxPooling3D((2, 2, 2))(c2)

c3 = Conv3D(64, (3, 3, 3), activation='relu',padding='same')(p2)
c3 = Dropout(0.2)(c3)
c3 = Conv3D(64, (3, 3, 3), activation='relu', padding='same')(c3)
p3 = MaxPooling3D((2, 2, 2))(c3)

c4 = Conv3D(128, (3, 3, 3), activation='relu', padding='same')(p3)
c4 = Dropout(0.2)(c4)
c4 = Conv3D(128, (3, 3, 3), activation='relu', padding='same')(c4)
p4 = MaxPooling3D(pool_size=(2, 2, 2))(c4)

c5 = Conv3D(256, (3, 3, 3), activation='relu', padding='same')(p4)
c5 = Dropout(0.3)(c5)
c5 = Conv3D(256, (3, 3, 3), activation='relu', padding='same')(c5)

#Expansive path
u6 = Conv3DTranspose(128, (2, 2, 2), strides=(2, 2, 2), padding='same')(c5)
u6 = concatenate([u6, c4])
c6 = Conv3D(128, (3, 3, 3), activation='relu', padding='same')(u6)
c6 = Dropout(0.2)(c6)
c6 = Conv3D(128, (3, 3, 3), activation='relu', padding='same')(c6)

u7 = Conv3DTranspose(64, (2, 2, 2), strides=(2, 2, 2), padding='same')(c6)
u7 = concatenate([u7, c3])
c7 = Conv3D(64, (3, 3, 3), activation='relu', padding='same')(u7)
c7 = Dropout(0.2)(c7)
c7 = Conv3D(64, (3, 3, 3), activation='relu', padding='same')(c7)

u8 = Conv3DTranspose(32, (2, 2, 2), strides=(2, 2, 2), padding='same')(c7)
u8 = concatenate([u8, c2])
c8 = Conv3D(32, (3, 3, 3), activation='relu', padding='same')(u8)
c8 = Dropout(0.1)(c8)
c8 = Conv3D(32, (3, 3, 3), activation='relu', padding='same')(c8)

u9 = Conv3DTranspose(16, (2, 2, 2), strides=(2, 2, 2), padding='same')(c8)
u9 = concatenate([u9, c1])
c9 = Conv3D(16, (3, 3, 3), activation='relu', padding='same')(u9)
c9 = Dropout(0.1)(c9)
c9 = Conv3D(16, (3, 3, 3), activation='relu', padding='same')(c9)

outputs = Conv3D(num_classes, (1, 1, 1), activation='softmax')(c9)
```

Fig. 6. Code Network architecture $128 \times 128 \times 128$, 4 channels, 3 classes

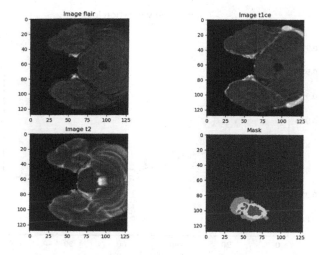

Fig. 7. Image Input to the model

More detailed Equation:

$$\text{DICE} = \frac{2\sum_{i=1}^{N} x_i y_i}{\sum_{i=1}^{N} x_i^2 + \sum_{i=1}^{N} y_i^2}$$

Where:

- DICE represents the Dice coefficient used as a similarity metric in image segmentation tasks. It measures the overlap between two sets.
- N is the total number of pixels in the images.
- x_i represents the value of the i-th pixel in the predicted segmentation image.
- y_i represents the value of the i-th pixel in the ground truth segmentation image.
- The summations $\sum_{i=1}^{N} x_i y_i$, $\sum_{i=1}^{N} x_i^2$, and $\sum_{i=1}^{N} y_i^2$ denote the sum of the cross products and sums of the squares of pixel values in both images.

For this reason, the present work is limited to presenting the data obtained for the competition using the proposed methodology, placing special emphasis on Fig. 10 that shows results of the new image size of $128 \times 128 \times 128$ different from the $240 \times 240 \times 155$ of the original image, and that Consequently, the number of parameters to be trained was reduced Fig. 9.

Finally, from a Dice Score of 0.2 (1 0.85) for training and 0.2 (1–0.80) for validation, Fig. 8, which was initially obtained for the model without data augmentation, after an iteration with the method a very significant improvement was obtained with a global average Table 2 of 0.42 ((0.43+0.48+0.36)/3) (Fig. 9).

The results show that the model obtained makes a correct segmentation. However, the dice score values are very low Fig. 8, compared to the State of

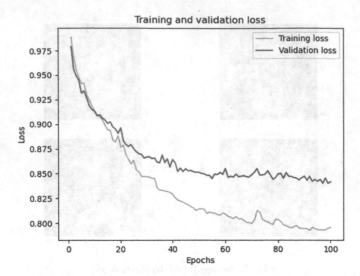

Fig. 8. The 3DUNet architecture training result.

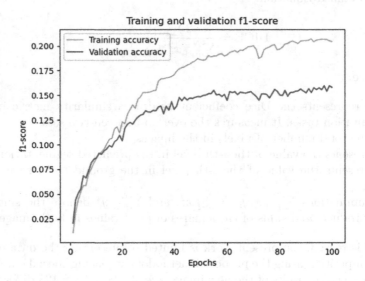

Fig. 9. The 3D-UNet architecture training result.

art [6]. In this case, it is not possible to determine whether this results from the trained model or the augmented data, considering that on the one hand, the number of model parameters was reduced and on the other hand, data augmentation of the images was made. Therefore, an open optimization problem remains between data-driven and model-driven tuning.

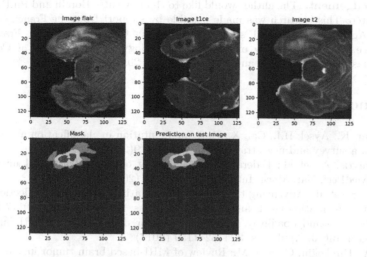

Fig. 10. Image Result model segmentation

Table 2. Final Model performance BraTS2023 challenge

scan_id	LesionWise_Score_Dice	LesionWise_Score_HD95	Sensitivity	Specificity
ET (Edema Tissue)				
mean	0.43	176.99	0.77	0.9995
std	0.32	136.07	0.26	0.0005
TC (Tumor Core)				
mean	0.48	168.20	0.81	0.9996
std	0.34	134.99	0.27	0.0008
WT (Whole Tumor)				
mean	0.36	225.36	0.92	0.9996
std	0.32	127.58	0.11	0.0018

5   Conclusion

A novel iterative data augmentation methodology has been presented combined
with scaling in the number of parameters of the neural network architecture, to
optimize results according to the specific segmentation problem. In other design
terms, it is the combination of a data-driven approach with a model-driven
approach to achieve an optimized solution.

   In future work, it is proposed to define an appropriate benchmark to evaluate this type of adaptive data-model-driven methodology to determine the true
impact of the technique on the general results of a baseline model.

Acknowledgement. The author would like to thank Centre Borelli and Ph.D.Miguel Colom Barco, This research was made possible by support from the French National Research Agency, the SESAME's OVD-SaaS project from Région Île de France and BPI France, and the Ministry of Science, Technology and Innovation of Colombia (Minciencias), call 885 of 2020 and Brats Challenge 2023.

References

1. Alomar, K., Aysel, H.I., Cai, X.: Data augmentation in classification and segmentation: a survey and new strategies. J. Imaging **9**(2), 46 (2023)
2. Karargyris, A., et al.: Federated benchmarking of medical artificial intelligence with MedPerf. Nat. Mach. Intell. **5**(7), 799–810 (2023)
3. Bakas, S., et al.: Advancing the cancer genome atlas glioma MRI collections with expert segmentation labels and radiomic features. Sci. Data **4**(1), 170117 (2017)
4. Ghosh, D., Bandyopadhyay, S.K.: Brain tumor detection from MRI image: an approach. Int. J. Appl. Res. **3**, 1152–1159 (2017)
5. Işın, A., Direkoğlu, C., Şah, M.: Review of MRI-based brain tumor image segmentation using deep learning methods. Procedia Comput. Sci. **102**, 317–324 (2016)
6. Pati, S., et al.: GaNDLF: the generally nuanced deep learning framework for scalable end-to-end clinical workflows. Commun. Eng. **2**(1), 23 (2023)
7. Shi, T., Jiang, H., Zheng, B.: A stacked generalization U-shape network based on zoom strategy and its application in biomedical image segmentation. Comput. Methods Programs Biomed. **197**, 105678 (2020)
8. Baid, U., et al.: The RSNA-ASNR-MICCAI BraTS 2021 Benchmark on Brain Tumor Segmentation and Radiogenomic Classification (2021). arXiv:2107.02314
9. Menze, B.H., et al.: The multimodal brain tumor image segmentation benchmark (BRATS). IEEE Trans. Med. Imaging **34**(10), 1993–2024 (2015)
10. Gao, M., Yu, R., Li, A., Morariu, V.I., Davis, L.S.: Dynamic zoom-in network for fast object detection in large images (2018)
11. Ding, F., et al.: Hierarchical Attention Networks for Medical Image Segmentation (2019). arXiv:1911.08777

Riemannian ElectroCardioGraphic Signal Classification

Aurélien Appriou[1] and Fabien Lotte[2](✉)

[1] Flit Sport, 20 rue Joseph Le Brix, 33000 Bordeaux, France
aurelien.appriou@flit-sport.fr
[2] Inria Center at the University of Bordeaux/LaBRI, 200 avenue de la Vieille Tour, 33400 Talence, France
fabien.lotte@inria.fr

Abstract. Estimating mental states such as cognitive workload from ElectroCardioGraphic (ECG) signals is a key but challenging step for many fields such as ergonomics, physiological computing, medical diagnostics or sport training. So far, the most commonly used machine learning algorithms to do so are linear classifiers such as Support Vector Machines (SVMs), often resulting in modest classification accuracies. However, Riemannian Geometry-based Classifiers (RGC), and more particularly the Tangent Space Classifiers (TSC), have recently shown to lead to state-of-the-art performances for ElectroEncephaloGraphic (EEG) signals classification. However, RGCs have never been explored for classifying ECG signals. Therefore, in this paper we design the first Riemannian geometry-based TSC for ECG signals, evaluate it for classifying two levels of cognitive workload, i.e., low versus high workload, and compare results to the ones obtained using an algorithm that is commonly used in the literature: the SVM. Our results indicated that the proposed ECG-TSC significantly outperformed an ECG-SVM classifier (a commonly used algorithm in the literature) when using 6, 10, 20, 30 and 40-s time windows, suggesting an optimal time window length of 120 s (65.3% classification accuracy for the TSC, 57.8% for the SVM). Altogether, our results showed the value of RGCs to process ECG signals, opening the door to many other promising ECG classification applications.

Keywords: Mental Workload · Machine Learning · Classification · Riemannian geometry · Electrocardiographic signals

1 Introduction

Monitoring users' mental states such as cognitive workload or affective states, in real time, has recently aroused a particular interest from fields such as neuroergonomics [26], Human Computer Interaction (HCI) [15] or passive Brain-Computer Interfaces (pBCI) [1,46]. Subjective measures, e.g., the NASA-TLX questionnaire [13], as well as behavioural measures, e.g., reaction time or error rate, have been used for assessing these mental states for a while. However, new methods using physiological sensors have been recently developed in order to bypass the lack of objectivity and the discontinuity of measurements of such

J. A. Riascos Salas et al. (Eds.): LAWCN 2023, CCIS 2108, pp. 25–39, 2024.
https://doi.org/10.1007/978-3-031-63848-0_3

methods. This field, known as "physiological computing" aims at extracting real-time information about users' states from physiological data such as heart rate, electrodermal activity or breathing [10].

Among the commonly used physiological sensors, ElectroCardioGraphy (ECG) has proven to be a useful signal in order to estimate mental states such as cognitive workload [11] or emotions [14]. In this paper, we focus in particular on the estimation of cognitive workload: based on the Cognitive Load Theory (CTL) [41], the cognitive workload is defined as the amount of cognitive/working memory resources that are necessary to process the information. While this mental state can be measured subjectively using questionnaires or estimated from behavioural measures, it can also be estimated physiologically [25]. This can enable continuous and objective mental workload estimation without interrupting the user. Among the various physiological signals that can be relevant for workload estimation, e.g., electrodermal activity [24], electroencephalogram [1] or electrooculogram [21], ECG was shown to be well related to cognitive workload and to be the most commonly used physiological measure to estimate it [7].

1.1   ECG Signal Classification Algorithms

If ECG has been widely used in the literature in order to study mental workload [7], the amount of studies that have attempted to estimate such a mental state using machine learning methods remains limited. Regarding ECG-based classification of mental workload levels, authors commonly focus on feature extraction methods, e.g., time domain and frequency domain-based features, combined with classical linear classifiers, e.g., Support Vector Machine (SVM) or Linear Discriminant Analysis (LDA). The time domain features include the descriptive statistics around the R-R interval (RRI), i.e., the interval between two successive heartbeats, or more precisely, the interval between two R peaks in the ECG signal [7], such as the standard deviation, the mean or the root mean square of these R-R intervals [38]. The frequency domain features are usually the power spectral densities in some frequency bands, e.g., the power spectral density of very low frequency band (0.003–0.040 Hz) to high frequency band (0.15–0.4 Hz), and power spectrum-based operations, e.g., the ratio, the normalization and/or the log transformation of various frequency band power. Additionally, non-linear features such as Poincarré plot, sample entropy or Shannon entropy can be used as well [6]. Concerning the classification methods that have been used for discriminating different levels of cognitive workload using ECG only, many machine learning algorithms have been used in the literature: SVM, LDA, K-Nearest Neighbor (KNN), Decision Tree (DT), Gentle Boost (GB), Naive Bayes (NB), Artificial Neural Network (ANN) and Logistic Regression (LR) [32,36,39]. Note that other algorithms can be used in the literature in order to classify ECG features combined with features from other sensors (Electroencephalography - EEG, skin conductance, etc). For example, some studies combined ECG with EEG features to classify workload levels, e.g., [16]. However, it did not result in reliable improvements when compared to the classification performance obtained from a single physiological signal.

1.2 ECG-Based Mental Workload Classification

In [12], authors applied a NB classifier on ECG data from twenty participants and obtained 76% of classification accuracy for discriminating low from high workload, levels that have been induced with elementary cognitive tasks [40]. In the same study, they applied a SVM with a cross-validation scheme on 30 participants using a 4-classes paradigm. Results showed a 80% classification accuracy. Authors chose to induce these 4 levels of cognitive workload using a combination of driving and N-back tasks, i.e., driving only vs driving with 3 different N-back task levels. Hogervorst & Brouwer applied both an Elastic Net (61% classification accuracy) and an SVM (55% classification accuracy) for discriminating two levels of workload (low vs high) [16]. These workload levels have been induced on 14 participants using the N-back task, and 120 s trials were fed to the algorithms. In [39], authors compared 5 classification algorithms in order to discriminate two levels of workload (low vs high) from 13 subjects using both driving and N-back tasks. The KNN significantly under-performed (71.5%) compared to ANN (74%), NB (74.1%) and LR (73.9%), but no difference was shown compare to DT (72.8%). In [47], authors applied a logistic regression in order to classify 2 levels of cognitive workload (low/high) and showed a average classification accuracy of 62.5% from 16 subjects. The high workload was induced by 6 different tasks, i.e., Go/No-go visual reaction, stroop, fast counting, speed run, visual forward digit span, and working memory tasks, whereas the low workload was based on a resting phase. Then, Tjolleng et al. designed an ANN in order to classify 3 states of workload, i.e., low, medium and high, induced using both simulated driving tasks and N-back tasks [43]. 15 subjects participated to the study whose results showed a classification accuracy reaching 82%. It is unfortunate though that this ANN was not compared to classical Machine Learning (ML) methods such as LDA or SVM. Parent et al. used a modified version of the N-back task, i.e., the Toulouse N-back task [20,30], in order to classify mental workload from ECG signals into 3 classes [27], using 22 types of features (e.g., time domain or frequency domain features). Results showed a classification accuracy of 42% with a NB classifier onto 18 participants. In [36], authors compared 6 classification methods on Hear Rate Variability (HRV) features from 6 subjects in order to discriminate 2 levels of workload (low vs high) from 3-minutes sliding windows of ECG using 10-fold cross-validation with a subject-specific calibration. Results showed that on average, the SVM, the KNN and the GB obtained classification accuracies above 95%, outperforming results from LDA (52.27%), NB (84.99%) and DT (89.91%). Note that the workload levels were induced with an interaction with a robot, resulting in 10 min of ECG recordings when the subject does not perform any task and maintains a relaxed state, and 10 min when the subject is asked to perform a complex task involving an interaction with the robot. In [32], authors focused on feature extraction in order to improve the classification accuracy in a two workload level paradigm, the levels being induced using the Multi-Attribute Task Battery (MATB-II, National Aeronautics and Space Administration (NASA), USA) [33]. They obtained 91% of classification accuracy by applying an SVM with a Radial Basis Function (RBF) kernel with cross-validation. Meteier et al. obtained 89% classification accuracy by applying a RF on ECG features in order to classify two levels of workload (low vs high) [22]. They used both a driving and an oral backward counting task [37] in order to induce different levels of workload from 90 participants.

In summary, most, if not all, of the features and machine learning algorithms cited in Sect. 1.1 were used to classify mental workload levels from ECG signals. Authors have used a number of workload inducing tasks such as N-back tasks [16], backward counting [22] or driving tasks [12], among others. Depending on the classifier used, the length of the time window of analysis and the mental workload inducing task, authors obtained accuracies between 55% to above 95% of accuracy, often around 75% on average, to discriminate two levels of workload, i.e., low versus high workload [12,16,22,32,36,39]. Studies that compared various classifiers together, suggested that SVM and ANN usually give state-of-the-art accuracies, and often outperform other algorithms such as LDA, NB or kNN [36,39]. Therefore, in this paper, we focus on the use of SVMs, both as a baseline state-of-the-art ECG classifier, and as a classifier used in the Riemannian Tangent Space of ECG covariance matrices, which we propose as a new classifier in this paper (see below for more details). We then compare this new Riemannian SVM ECG classifier to the classical use of SVM applied to euclidean ECG feature vectors.

1.3   Paper Objectives

The accuracies obtained so far for classifying cognitive workload levels, mostly around 75% from long time windows (usually several minutes), revealed the need for more robust and accurate ECG classification algorithms in order to obtain trustable ECG-based cognitive load estimators. Therefore, we propose in this paper to explore a type of algorithms that proved very effective for EEG classification, but that has never been studied, to the best of our knowledge, for ECG classification: Riemannian Geometry-based Tangent Space Classifiers (TSC) [1,4,45]. Such family of algorithms represents EEG signals as Symmetric Positive Definite (SPD) matrices, typically covariance matrices, and then directly classify such matrices using Riemannian geometry. This last few years, Riemannian Geometry Classifiers (RGCs) have been shown to be the state-of-the-art EEG signal classification algorithms, winning the vast majority of international brain signal classification competitions [9,17,34,45]. Their effectiveness is thought to be due to 1) their small numbers of parameters, which enables them to be trainable from little training data and 2) the invariance properties of the Riemannian distance (which is invariant to full rank linear transformations) used in RGCs, which enables RGCs to be naturally robust to some variabilities affecting EEG signals [9,34,45]. ECG and EEG signals share numerous properties, notably both are biomedical electrical time series, both suffer from various variabilities and classifiers of both signals usually need to be calibrated from little training data. Thus, it seems promising to explore RGCs for ECG signals classification as well. Therefore, in this paper, we first propose a novel representation of ECG signals as SPD matrices. We then assess how well a Riemannian TSC could classify such ECG SPD matrices, and compared it to euclidean SVM ECG classifiers used as baselines. In this paper, we first present the workload data set used, then the ECG features we extracted as well as the machine learning algorithms employed. We used a subject-specific design - with each algorithm trained on data specific to each subject - and we then tested them on different data from the same subject - using a 5-fold cross-validation.

2   Materials and Methods

2.1   Mental Workload Data Set

The data set used for this study comes from [23], which conducted a workload inducing experiment on 22 subjects, while collecting physiological signals such as EEG (the initial focus of that paper) and ECG. Consent forms had been filled-in and signed by the subjects in the original paper study. Among those subjects, only 13 had usable ECG signals so we ran our ECG study on these 13 subjects. In the experiment, mental workload variations have been induced using N-back tasks. With such tasks, users saw a sequence of letters on screen, the letters being displayed one by one, every 2 s. For each letter the user had to indicate with a mouse click whether the displayed letter was the same one as the letter displayed N letters before. Users alternated between easy blocks ("low" workload label) with the 0-back task (the user had to identify whether the current letter was the letter 'X') and difficult blocks ("high" workload label) with the 2-back task (the user had to identify whether the current letter was the same letter as the one displayed 2 letters before) to reach a total of 24 blocks. Each block of 120 s was labeled with its workload level: "low" workload for 0-back trials and "high" workload for 2-back trials. Note that a short break was taken after each 6 blocks, but not between each block. This could generate an additional workload to both low and high workload conditions due to the accumulated fatigue. Each block of 120 s was then split later on using 6, 10, 20, 30, 40, 60 or 120-s long time windows, resulting in the creation of 7 different data sets for our study. This splitting aimed at assessing the time window length influence on mental workload estimation quality from ECG signals. Signals from two ECG electrodes, 28 EEG electrodes, two facial ElectroMyoGram (EMG), four ElectroOculoGram (EOG), breath belt, pulse and a galvanic skin response sensor have been collected, all with a g.USBAmp (g.tec, Austria) and associated sensors. For our study, we kept ECG signals only, and assessed the performances of both classification algorithms (the proposed Riemannian TSC and the baseline euclidean SVMs) using a within-participant study with five-fold stratified Cross-Validation. This means that the data from each participant was divided into five parts: four parts were used for training the classifier and the fifth one for testing the resulting classifier for that participant. This process was repeated five times, with each part used exactly once as the testing set.

2.2   Feature Extraction

In order to estimate workload levels from ECG signals, we investigated two different machine learning algorithms, i.e., an Euclidean SVM and a RGC-TSC, both using the same ECG features, i.e., time, frequency and nonlinear domain-based features [31], represented classically as a feature vector for the Euclidean SVM, or as a newly proposed SPD matrix for the RGC-TSC. We thus first extracted the following 34 ECG features using neurokit [18]:

- *sdRR:* the standard deviation of the RRIs [38].
- *meanRR:* the mean of the RRI [44].
- *RMSSD:* the Root Mean Square of the RRIs [38].
- *CVSD:* the Coefficient of Variation of Successive Differences. This corresponds to the RMSSD divided by meanRR [19].
- *cvRR:* the RR coefficient of variation. This corresponds to the sdRR divided by the meanRR [19].
- *medianRR:* the median of the absolute values of the RRIs' successsive differences [44].
- *madRR:* the RRIs' median absolute deviation [19].
- *mcvRR:* the RRIs' median-based coefficient of variation. This corresponds to the ratio of madRR divided by medianRR [44].
- *RR50 or RR20:* the successive RRIs' number of interval differences greater than 50ms or 20 ms, respectively [19].
- *pRR50 or pRR20:* the proportion derived by dividing RR50 (ou RR20) by the number of RRIs [44].
- *triang:* the HRV triangular index measurement, i.e., plotting the integral of the ratio of RRI density histogram by its height [35].
- *Shannon_h:* the Shannon entropy calculated from the class probabilities of the RRI density distribution [44].
- *VLF:* the HRV variance in the Very Low Frequency (0.003 to 0.04 Hz) [19].
- *LF:* the HRV variance in the Low Frequency (0.04 to 0.15 Hz) [19,44].
- *HF:* the HRV variance in the High Frequency (0.15 to 0.40 Hz) [19,44].
- *Total_Power*: the total power of the density spectra [44].
- *LFHF:* the LF/HF ratio [19,44].
- *LFn:* the normalized LF power. It can be calculated using the equation "LFn = LF/(LF+HF)" [19].
- *HFn:* the normalized HF power. It can be calculated using the equation "HFn = HF/(LF+HF)" [19].
- *LFp:* the LF/Total_Power ratio [44].
- *HFp:* the HF/Total_Power ratio [44].
- *DFA:* the Detrended Fluctuation Analysis (DFA) [2] of the heart rate raw signals.
- *Shannon:* the RRIs' Shannon entropy [44].
- *sample_entropy:* the RRIs' sample entropy [42].
- *correlation_Dimension:* RRIs' correlation dimension [44].
- *entropy_Multiscale:* the RRIs' entropy multiscale [42].

- *entropy_ SVD:* the RRIs' Singular Value Decomposition (SVD) entropy [44].
- *entropy_ Spectral_ VLF:* the RRIs' Spectral Entropy (SE) over the VLF [44].
- *entropy_ Spectral_ LF:* the RRIs' SE over the LF [44].
- *entropy_ Spectral_ HF:* the RRIs' SE over the HF [44].
- *Fisher_ Info:* the RRIs' Fisher information [2].
- *Lyapunov:* the RRIs' Lyapunov exponent [2].
- *FD_ Petrosian:* RRIs' Petrosian's Fractal Dimension [2].
- *FD_ Higushi:* the RRI Higushi's Fractal Dimension [2].

2.3   Machine Learning Algorithms

As mentioned earlier, we compared two ECG classification methods: a classical Euclidean SVM and the proposed Riemannian Geometry-based TSC. We describe how they are used below.

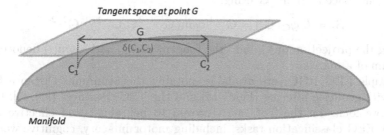

Fig. 1. Schematic representation of a Riemannian manifold with matrix G, the Riemannian average of covariance matrices C_1 and C_2. The tangent space to the Riemannian manifold at point G is represented in red.

Euclidean Support Vector Machine. Among the 34 features described above, the ten most relevant ones for classification were selected using the minimal Redundancy Maximal Relevance (mRMR) feature selection algorithm [29], arranged as a vector and used to train and test a standard Euclidean SVM classifier. Note that we ran the SVM with two types of kernels, i.e., a linear kernel and a Radial Basis Function (RBF) kernel. We refer to them as SVM_{linear} and SVM_{RBF}, respectively. We used default hyperparameters ($C = 1.0$) from scikit-learn [28].

Riemannian Geometry Classifiers. As mentioned, RGCs proved to be very effective for EEG-based classification of mental states, reaching state-of-the-art performances [1,4,34,45], but, to the best of our knowledge, have never been used for the classification of ECG signals yet. In this section, we first introduce the general concepts of RGCs as it is established for EEG classification, before presenting how we adapted a particular RGC, the TSC, to classify ECG.

Riemannian Geometry General Concepts. In EEG Riemannian approaches, EEG trials are represented as covariance matrices - more specifically as symmetric positive definite (SPD) matrices - these matrices being manipulated with an appropriate geometry, the Riemannian geometry [4,45]. With such a geometry, the *intrinsic* non-Euclidean distance between two SPD matrices, i.e. the distance between two points (here $\mathbf{C}_1$ and $\mathbf{C}_2$) on the Riemannian *manifold*, can be estimated using the Riemannian distance δ^2:

$$\delta^2(\mathbf{C}_1, \mathbf{C}_2) = \|\log(C_1^{-\frac{1}{2}}C_2C_1^{-\frac{1}{2}})\|_F = \left(\sum_{i=1}^{n}\log^2\lambda_i\right)^{1/2} \tag{1}$$

where λ_i are the eigenvalues of $C_1^{-\frac{1}{2}}C_2C_1^{-\frac{1}{2}}$ and $\|.\|_F$ the Frobenius norm. On the *manifold*, the set of tangent vectors to point $\mathbf{G}$ defines the manifold tangent space at $\mathbf{G}$. Figure 1 shows the tangent space at point $\mathbf{G}$, which is the centroid (mean) of $\mathbf{C}_1$ and $\mathbf{C}_2$. More generally, any SPD matrix $\mathbf{C}_i$ can be projected onto the tangent space at point $\mathbf{G}$ using:

$$\mathbf{S}_i = Log_{\mathbf{G}}(\mathbf{C}_i) = \mathbf{G}^{1/2}logm(\mathbf{G}^{-1/2}\mathbf{C}_i\mathbf{G}^{-1/2})\mathbf{G}^{1/2} \tag{2}$$

$\mathbf{S}_i$ being the projection of $\mathbf{C}_i$ onto the tangent plane, and $logm(\cdot)$ denoting the logarithm of a matrix.

Multiple EEG RGCs are available, notably the Minimum Distance to the Mean with geodesic filtering (FgMDM) and the TSC classifiers [1,4,45]. In this article, we focus on the TSC as it proved to be robust and effective across multiple EEG classification tasks, including motor imagery, cognitive workload and affective state EEG-based classification [2].

Tangent Space Classifier. TSC projects SPD matrices $\mathbf{C}_i$ onto the tangent space at point $\mathbf{G}$ (the training data mean) using Eq. (2), to obtain matrices $\mathbf{S}_i$. Then, it uses any classifier such as LDA or SVM on the vectorized upper-triangular elements of the projected matrices [4]. In this paper, we used the exact same SVMs as for the classical ECG SVM classifiers (Sect. 2.3), with the same hyperparameters, for a fair comparison.

TSC for ECG Signals Classification. In our study, we revisited this EEG Riemannian classifier approach, i.e., the TSC, and adapted it to ECG signals. To do so, we first followed a two-step approach in order to represent ECG features as an SPD Matrix. First, we bandpass filtered the ECG into the 4 frequency bands described in Sect. 2.2, i.e., VLF (0.003 to 0.04 Hz), LF (0.04 to 0.15 Hz), HF (0.15 to 0.40 Hz), as well as the total power (TP, 0.003 to 40 Hz). We then computed the covariance matrix of these four frequency-specific ECG signals, leading to a 4×4 covariance matrix. Second, we extended this 4×4 matrix using 0 s in order to obtain a 10×10 matrix, the number 10 corresponding to the 4 frequency bands above in addition to the 6 most relevant features[1] (selected using mRMR

---

[1] Note that the feature extraction and selection was intra-subject (a.k.a. subject specific) and not inter-subject, hence the selected features are not presented here. Indeed, different features were selected for different subjects.

as for the classical Euclidean SVM) among the other features described above (see Sect. 2.2), i.e., the time, frequency and nonlinear domain-based features. We then added the values of the extracted features (except the ones already represented as covariance matrix, i.e., VLF, LF, HF and TP) onto the diagonal (from the 5th to the 10th diagonal element) of this 10×10 matrix. This lead to a SPD matrix using 10 feature types, i.e., as many as the classical Euclidean SVM pipeline above. We finally use this new type of SPD matrix to represent ECG signals with the TSC classifier.

3   Results

The average classification accuracies obtained with each classifier and time window to classify low versus high mental workload from ECG are reported in Figs. 1 and 2. As a reference, the statistical chance levels using [8] were estimated at 51.04% (480 trials), 51.33% (290 trials), 51.88% (145 trials), 52.31% (100 trials), 52.62% (75 trials), 53.23% (50 trials), as well as 54.46% (25 trials) for respectively the 6, 10, 20, 30, 40, 60 and 120-s long time windows, all for 13 subjects. We used a 2-way ANOVA with repeated measures to evaluate the performances of factor *time windows* according to factor *algorithms* ($TSC_{SVMlinear}$ vs TSC_{SVMRBF} vs SVM_{linear} vs SVM_{RBF}). Note that we checked data sphericity and normality, and used Greenhouse-Geisser (GG) correction if needed.

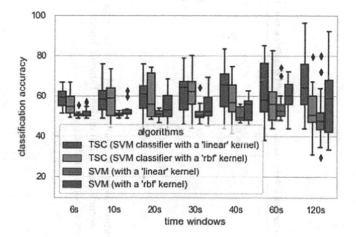

Fig. 2. Classification accuracy for each time window and algorithm, i.e., (Euclidean) SVM with both 'linear' and 'RBF' kernels and (Riemannian) TSC with an SVM classifier using both 'linear' and 'RBF' kernels.

The ANOVA revealed a main effect of *algorithms* [GG(1,13) = 11.17, p = 0.0008] and for *algorithms*time windows* [F(1,13) = 1.776, p = 0.029], but not for *time windows* [GG(1,13) = 1.115, p = 0.350]. Post-hoc analyses results

	TSC (SVM classifier with a 'linear' kernel)	TSC (SVM classifier with a 'rbf' kernel)	SVM (with a 'linear' kernel)	SVM (with a 'rbf' kernel)	chance level
6s	58.3 (5.0)	56.0 (5.4)	50.7 (1.6)	51.4 (2.8)	51.04
10s	59.3 (8.4)	57.7 (8.7)	50.6 (1.2)	52.8 (3.9)	51.33
20s	60.0 (10.5)	60.0 (11.0)	50.8 (2.0)	54.4 (7.1)	51.88
30s	61.2 (10.5)	61.4 (11.4)	51.7 (4.7)	54.8 (7.9)	52.31
40s	62.2 (11.7)	58.4 (10.1)	50.9 (3.4)	53.5 (6.3)	52.62
60s	62.4 (14.7)	56.5 (10.7)	55.4 (8.2)	60.5 (9.2)	53.23
120s	65.3 (15.6)	52.0 (13.9)	50.4 (14.2)	57.8 (19.5)	54.46

Table 1. Mean classification accuracy (and standard deviation) for each algorithm, i.e., Euclidean Support Vector Machine (SVM) with both 'linear' and 'RBF' kernels and Riemannian Tangent Space Classifier (TSC) with a SVM classifier using both 'linear' and 'RBF' kernels, and for each time window length.

using Student t-test with False Discovery Rate (FDR) corrections showed significant differences between $TSC_{SVMlinear}$, TSC_{SVMRBF}, SVM_{linear} and SVM_{RBF} when using different times windows lengths. Here, we focus on the differences observed between the $TSC_{SVMlinear}$ and SVM_{linear}, as well as the differences observed between the TSC_{SVMRBF} and the SVM_{RBF}. Interestingly enough, the Riemannian $TSC_{SVMlinear}$ outperformed the Euclidean SVM_{linear} for the 6 s [$p \leq 0.05$], 10 s [$p \leq 0.05$], 20 s [$p \leq 0.05$], 30 s [$p \leq 0.05$] and 40 s [$p \leq 0.05$] time windows. The same post-hoc analyses showed that the Riemannian TSC_{SVMRBF} also outperformed the Euclidean SVM_{RBF} for the 6 s [$p \leq 0.05$] time window. Finally, the comparison between the $TSC_{SVMlinear}$ and the TSC_{SVMRBF} showed a significant difference for the 120 s [$p \leq 0.05$] time window. The $TSC_{SVMlinear}$ outperformed chance level on all time windows (Fig. 3).

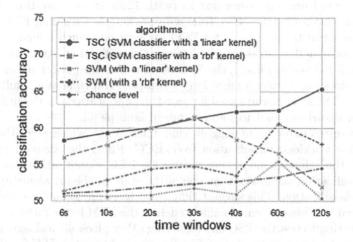

Fig. 3. Classification accuracy for each time window and algorithm, i.e., Euclidean SVM with both 'linear' and 'RBF' kernels and Riemannian TSC with an SVM classifier using both 'linear' and 'RBF' kernels.

4   Discussion and Conclusion

In this paper, we studied an effective EEG classifier, the Riemannian Geometry TSC, and adapted it for classifying ECG, here to estimate different levels of cognitive workload. We notably proposed a new representation of ECG as an SPD matrix. We compared the results obtained by the proposed ECG-TSC to those of a widely used state-of-the-art ECG classifier, i.e., an Euclidean SVM, based on the same ECG features. We assessed such algorithms for multiple time window lengths, on an ECG data set from [23], where 0 and 2-back tasks have been used to induce low and high levels of workload.

First, the (Riemannian) $TSC_{SVMlinear}$ obtained better performances than the (Euclidean) SVM_{linear} for all time windows, and even significantly outperformed this SVM_{linear} as well as the chance level when using 6, 10, 20, 30 and 40-s long time windows, with respectively 58.3%, 59.3%, 60.0%, 61.2% and 62.2% classification accuracy versus 50.7%, 50.6%, 50.8%, 51.7% and 50.9% for the SVM_{linear}. The TSC_{SVMRBF} also outperformed the SVM_{RBF} with 56.0% classification accuracy versus 51.4%.

All together, these results highlight the potential of TSC for classifying ECG signals, here for estimating cognitive workload, which could prove useful for ergonomics, HCI or medical diagnostic among others. Another relevant result about the TSC itself is that, among the two types of studied kernels for the TSC-SVM, the 'linear' one obtained the best scores on most time windows, and significantly outperformed the 'RBF' kernel for the 120 s time window (65.3% vs 52.0%). Finally, it is worth noting that the Riemannian TSC was able to train ECG classifiers from only a few dozens (with 120 s or 60 s long time windows) or a few hundreds (for the other time window lengths) training ECG trials, a typical number of training trials for ECG applications. Such a number of trials would be too small for training data hungry classification algorithms such as Deep Neural Networks. Finally, the TSC obtained better performances than the SVM, but does not require a much longer computation time as a result. Indeed, RGC-based TSCs are already used for real-time applications in the field of BCI, with larger covariance matrices and standard laptops [5].

Such results enable us to suggest guidelines about which algorithm to use for cognitive workload classification from ECG. First, the Riemannian Geometry TSC, that showed interesting results for EEG classification, also showed better classification accuracies than one of the state-of-the-art algorithm (SVM) for ECG classification. This suggest that this algorithm should be preferred to vector-based Euclidean linear classifiers such as the SVM in the future. Moreover, it be interesting to test the TSC for classifying other physiological signals such as electrodermal activity or breathing. Finally, we used here the TSC for classifying cognitive workload levels, but EEG-RGCs showed promising results for classifying other mental states such as epistemic curiosity or emotions [1,3]. It would thus be interesting to study the use of TSC to classify epistemic curiosity or emotion levels from ECG as well. Altogether our results show that Riemannian geometry classifiers appear to be very promising for ECG signal classification as well, as such, should be explored deeper for that field as well.

Acknowledgments. This work was supported by the European Research Council (grant ERC-2016-STG-714567).

References

1. Appriou, A., Cichocki, A., Lotte, F.: Modern machine learning algorithms to classify cognitive and affective states from electroencephalography signals. IEEE SMC Mag. 1–8 (2020)
2. Appriou, A., Pillette, L., Trocellier, D., Dutartre, D., Cichocki, A., Lotte, F.: Biopyc, an open-source python toolbox for offline electroencephalographic and physiological signals classification. Sensors **21** (2021). https://doi.org/10.3390/s21175740
3. Appriou, A., Ceha, J., Pramij, S., Dutartre, D., Law, E., Oudeyer, P.Y., Lotte, F.: Towards measuring states of epistemic curiosity through electroencephalographic signals. In: 2020 IEEE International Conference on Systems, Man, and Cybernetics (SMC), pp. 4006–4011. IEEE (2020)
4. Barachant, A., Bonnet, S., Congedo, M., Jutten, C.: Multiclass brain-computer interface classification by Riemannian geometry. IEEE Trans. Biomed. Eng. **59**(4), 920–928 (2012)
5. Benaroch, C., et al.: Long-term BCI training of a tetraplegic user: adaptive riemannian classifiers and user training. Front. Hum. Neurosci. **15**, 635653 (2021). https://doi.org/10.3389/fnhum.2021.635653
6. Castaldo, R., Montesinos, L., Wan, T.S., Serban, A., Massaro, S., Pecchia, L.: Heart rate variability analysis and performance during a repeated mental workload task. In: EMBEC/NBC -2017. IP, vol. 65, pp. 69–72. Springer, Singapore (2018). https://doi.org/10.1007/978-981-10-5122-7_18
7. Charles, R., Nixon, J.: Measuring mental workload using physiological measures: a systematic review. Appl. Ergon. (2018). https://doi.org/10.1016/j.apergo.2018.08.028
8. Combrisson, E., Jerbi, K.: Exceeding chance level by chance: the caveat of theoretical chance levels in brain signal classification and statistical assessment of decoding accuracy. J. Neurosci. Methods **250**, 126–136 (2015)
9. Congedo, M., Barachant, A., Bhatia, R.: Riemannian geometry for EEG-based brain-computer interfaces; a primer and a review. Brain-Comput. Interfaces **4**(3), 155–174 (2017)
10. Fairclough, S.: Fundamentals of physiological computing. Interact. Comput. **21**, 133–145 (2009). https://doi.org/10.1016/j.intcom.2008.10.011
11. Fairclough, S., Houston, K.: A metabolic measure of mental effort. Biol. Psychol. **66**, 177–90 (2004). https://doi.org/10.1016/j.biopsycho.2003.10.001
12. Haapalainen Ferreira, E., Kim, S., Forlizzi, J., Dey, A.: Psycho-physiological measures for assessing cognitive load, pp. 301–310 (2010). https://doi.org/10.1145/1864349.1864395
13. Hart, S.: Nasa-task load index (NASA-TLX); 20 years later. Proc. Hum. Factors Ergon. Soc. Annu. Meet. **50** (2006). https://doi.org/10.1177/154193120605000909
14. Hasnul, M., Aziz, N.A., Alelyani, S., Mohana, M., Aziz, A.A.: Electrocardiogram-based emotion recognition systems and their applications in healthcare-a review. Sensors **21**, 5015 (2021). https://doi.org/10.3390/s21155015
15. Hewett, T., et al.: ACM SIGCHI curricula for human-computer interaction. WWW Document (1992)
16. Hogervorst, M., Brouwer, A.M., Erp, J.: Combining and comparing EEG, peripheral physiology and eye-related measures for the assessment of mental workload. Front. Neurosci. **8**, 322 (2014). https://doi.org/10.3389/fnins.2014.00322

17. Lotte, F., et al.: A review of classification algorithms for EEG-based brain-computer interfaces: a 10 year update. J. Neural Eng. **15**(3), 031005 (2018)
18. Makowski, D., et al.: Neurokit2: a python toolbox for neurophysiological signal processing. BRM (2021). https://doi.org/10.3758/s13428-020-01516-y
19. Malik, M.: Heart rate variability: standards of measurement, physiological interpretation, and clinical use. Circulation **93**, 1043–1065 (1996)
20. Mandrick, K., Peysakhovich, V., Rémy, F., Lepron, E., Causse, M.: Neural and psychophysiological correlates of human performance under stress and high mental workload. Biol. Psychol. **121** (2016). https://doi.org/10.1016/j.biopsycho.2016.10.002
21. Marquart, G., Cabrall, C., de Winter, J.: Review of eye-related measures of drivers' mental workload. Procedia Manufact. (2015). https://doi.org/10.1016/j.promfg.2015.07.783
22. Meteier, Q., et al.: Classification of drivers' workload using physiological signals in conditional automation. Front. Psychol. **12**, 596038 (2021). https://doi.org/10.3389/fpsyg.2021.596038
23. Mühl, C., Jeunet, C., Lotte, F.: EEG-based workload estimation across affective contexts. Front. Neurosci. **8**, 1–15 (2014)
24. Nourbakhsh, N., Chen, F., Wang, Y., Calvo, R.: Detecting users' cognitive load by galvanic skin response with affective interference. ACM Trans. Interact. Intell. Syst. **7**, 1–20 (2017). https://doi.org/10.1145/2960413
25. O'Donnell, R.D.: Workload assessment methodology. Cognitive Processes and Performance (1986). https://ci.nii.ac.jp/naid/10021915444/en/
26. Parasuraman, R., Wilson, G.: Putting the brain to work: neuroergonomics past, present, and future. Hum. Factors **50**(3), 468–474 (2008)
27. Parent, M., Peysakhovich, V., Mandrick, K., Tremblay, S., Causse, M.: The diagnosticity of psychophysiological signatures: can we disentangle mental workload from acute stress with ECG and FNIRS? Int. J. Psychophysiol. **146** (2019). https://doi.org/10.1016/j.ijpsycho.2019.09.005
28. Pedregosa, F., et al.: Scikit-learn: machine learning in python. J. Mach. Learn. Res. **12** (2011). https://dl.acm.org/citation.cfm?id=2078195
29. Peng, H., Long, F., Ding, C.: Feature selection based on mutual information: criteria of max-dependency, max-relevance, and min-redundancy. IEEE Trans. Pattern Anal. Mach. Intell. **27**, 1226–1238 (2005)
30. Peysakhovich, V., Vachon, F., Dehais, F.: The impact of luminance on tonic and phasic pupillary responses to sustained cognitive load. Int. J. Psychophysiol. **112**, 40–45 (2017). https://doi.org/10.1016/j.ijpsycho.2016.12.003
31. Pham, T., Lau, Z.J., Chen, S., Makowski, D.: Heart rate variability in psychology: a review of HRV indices and an analysis tutorial. Sensors **21** (2021). https://doi.org/10.3390/s21123998
32. Qu, H., Gao, X., Pang, L.: Classification of mental workload based on multiple features of ECG signals. Inform. Med. Unlocked **24**, 100575 (2021). https://doi.org/10.1016/j.imu.2021.100575
33. Qu, H., et al.: Mental workload classification method based on EEG independent component features. Appl. Sci. **10**, 3036 (2020). https://doi.org/10.3390/app10093036
34. Roy, R.N., et al.: Retrospective on the first passive brain-computer interface competition on cross-session workload estimation. Front. Neuroergonomics 4 (2022)
35. Shaffer, F., Ginsberg, J.P.: An overview of heart rate variability metrics and norms. Front. Public Health **5**, 258 (2017). https://doi.org/10.3389/fpubh.2017.00258

36. Shao, S., Wang, T., Wang, Y., Su, Y., Song, C., Yao, C.: Research of HRV as a measure of mental workload in human and dual-arm robot interaction. Electronics **9**, 2174 (2020). https://doi.org/10.3390/electronics9122174
37. Siegenthaler, E., et al.: Task difficulty in mental arithmetic affects microsaccadic rates and magnitudes. Eur. J. Neurosci. **39**, 287–94 (2014). https://doi.org/10.1111/ejn.12395
38. Smith, A.L., Owen, H., Reynolds, K.: Heart rate variability indices for very short-term (30 beat) analysis. Part 1: survey and toolbox. J. Clin. Monit. Comput. **15** (2013)
39. Solovey, E., Zec, M., Garcia Perez, E., Reimer, B., Mehler, B.: Classifying driver workload using physiological and driving performance data: two field studies. In: Conference on Human Factors in Computing Systems - Proceedings (2014). https://doi.org/10.1145/2556288.2557068
40. Stanton, N.: Human cognitive abilities: a survey of factor-analytic studies, by J. B. Carroll. Ergonomics **38** (2007). https://doi.org/10.1080/00140139508925174
41. Sweller, J., Van Merrienboer, J.J.G., Paas, F.: Cognitive architecture and instructional design. Educ. Psych. Rev. **10**, 251–296 (1998). https://doi.org/10.1023/a:1022193728205
42. Tiwari, A., et al.: Multi-scale heart beat entropy measures for mental workload assessment of ambulant users. Entropy **21**(8), 1–20 (2019). https://doi.org/10.3390/e21080783
43. Tjolleng, A., et al.: Classification of a driver's cognitive workload levels using artificial neural network on ECG signals. Appl. Ergon. (2017). https://doi.org/10.1016/j.apergo.2016.09.013
44. Voss, A., Schroeder, R., Heitmann, A., Peters, A., Perz, S.: Short-term heart rate variability - influence of gender and age in healthy subjects. PLoS ONE **10**(3), 1–33 (2015). https://doi.org/10.1371/journal.pone.0118308
45. Yger, F., Berar, M., Lotte, F.: Riemannian approaches in brain-computer interfaces: a review. IEEE TNSRE **25**(10), 1753–1762 (2016)
46. Zander, T., Kothe, C.: Towards passive brain-computer interfaces: applying brain-computer interface technology to human-machine systems in general. J. Neur. Eng. **8**, 025005 (2011)
47. Zhang, H., Zhu, Y., Jayachandran, M., Guan, C.: Detection of variations in cognitive workload using multi-modality physiological sensors and a large margin unbiased regression machine, vol. 2014 (2014).https://doi.org/10.1109/EMBC.2014.6944250

Computational Neuroscience

Evaluation of Wnt/β-Catenin Pathway Modulation on CA3-CA1 Synaptic Plasticity Model: An Aproximation to Alzheimer Disease

Hernán Villota[1]([⊠]) and Karla Avilez[2]

[1] Faculty of Engineering, University Institution of Envigado,
Carrera 27B # 39A Sur 57, Envigado 055422, Antioquia, Colombia
hdvillota@correo.iue.edu.co
[2] Department of Cognitive Neuroscience, Institute of Cellular Physiology, UNAM,
Circuito Exterior s/n Ciudad Universitaria, Coyoacán 04510, Cd. México, México

Abstract. Introduction: The Wnt/β-Catenin pathway is associated with embryogenesis, cell proliferation, and tissue modulation, and its impairment is linked to some pathologies such as cancer. Recent studies have suggested that this signaling pathway is implicated in the genesis and progression of neurodegenerative diseases like Alzheimer's disease (AD) in a multi-mechanistic way, for example affecting synaptic plasticity processes through the regulation of amyloidβ (Aβ) levels, a peptide closely related to AD development. In this context, the development and implementation of computational models of these molecular pathway and its interaction with synaptic plasticity process are valuable tools that could aid in understanding the underlying mechanisms of these complex processes.

Methods: In this study, we propose to model the impact of regulation Aβ levels by activating or deactivating the Wnt/β-Catenin pathway over a previously reported synaptic plasticity computational model developed by Dainauskas et al. (2023) [8]. For the Wnt/β-Catenin pathway model, we implemented differential equations in Python to analyze five key elements of the pathway in the context of AD: Wnt, GSK3-β, β-Catenin, BACE1 gene, and Amyloid-β. The proposed methodology includes the implementation of Python code with NEURON libraries. For the evaluation of the effect, membrane potential, NMDA receptor conductance and synapse weight will be measured in different conditions of WNT/Aß levels, based in concentrations reported in vitro studies.

Results: We evaluated different levels of Wnt, the dynamics of the Wnt pathway model were adapted to in vitro experimental results. Also the connection with the synaptic plasticity model shows the influence of Wnt levels on the modulation of synaptic weight through the regulation of NMDA receptor conductance levels. When we analyse each element in the pathway in our model we validate that these elements had a consistent behaviour according to experimental data. This model recreates an in silico approximation of the Wnt pathway and its relationship with synaptic plasticity process.

J. A. Riascos Salas et al. (Eds.): LAWCN 2023, CCIS 2108, pp. 43–56, 2024.
https://doi.org/10.1007/978-3-031-63848-0_4

Keywords: Plasticity · Amyloid-β · Alzheimer · Wnt/β-Catenin pathway

1   Introduction

Understanding synaptic plasticity, the fundamental mechanism underpinning learning and memory, is a complex yet crucial aspect of neuroscience. Computational models play a pivotal role in unraveling the intricacies of synaptic function, bridging molecular insights with system-level behavior. Antecedents in this field have contributed diverse computational approaches, ranging from phenomenological models to biophysical simulations [1].

Synaptic plasticity, particularly in the hippocampal CA3-CA1 circuit, heavily relies on the intricate dynamics of N-methyl-D-aspartate receptors (NMDARs). These receptors, composed of various subunits such as GluN2B and GluN2A, modulate long-term potentiation (LTP) and long-term depression (LTD), respectively. These procces are related with a sustained increase/decrease in glutamatergic synaptic efficacy that follow in response to discrete patterns of presynaptic firing [2,3]. The GluN2B-NMDAR subunit, in particular, has emerged as a critical player, impacting synaptic strength and cognitive functions. Deregulation of GluN2B-NMDAR has been implicated in conditions such as Alzheimer's disease, disrupting synaptic plasticity and cognitive processes. In the realm of neurodegenerative diseases, Alzheimer's disease takes center stage. The pathological accumulation of amyloidß (Aß) peptide, a derivative of amyloid precursor protein (APP), is a hallmark of Alzheimer's progression. Disruptions in synaptic plasticity, attributed to altered NMDAR function, are intricately linked to the cognitive decline observed in Alzheimer's patients [4]

In the context of the Wnt/β-Catenin pathway, a highly studied signaling cascade known for its involvement in embryogenesis, cellular division, and tissue regulation. Recent findings suggest its significant role in Alzheimer's, specifically in modulating Aβ levels. The pathway's activation appears to inhibit the expression of a protein associated with APP synthesis, thereby influencing Aβ production. In this intricate interplay, Wnt/β-Catenin emerges as a potential regulator of Aβ levels, offering a novel alternative for therapeutic exploration [5].

Wnt/β-Catenin Pathway in AD:
In a summarized manner, this molecular pathway contain key elements with specific roles. First, the Wnt ligand acts as an inductor or activator of the pathway. Second, the β-Catenin protein acts as an effector through the regulation of gene expression. Third, the β-Catenin degradation complex, a protein complex that includes key proteins such as Axin, GSK3-β, and APC, regulates the levels of β-Catenin through degradation. In the Off state of the pathway without Wnt, the β-Catenin degradation complex mark β-Catenin protein to its proteosomal degradation in cytosol, inhibiting its activity as a gene expression regulator. On the other hand, in the On state with presence of Wnt, the β-Catenin degradation complex is inhibited. In consequence, β-Catenin levels increase in the cytosol and

β-Catenin is capable of translocating to nucleus, where acts as a gene expression regulator by binding with the transcription factor TCF [6]. A representative graph of this mechanism can be seen in Fig. 1A. In Alzheimer's disease (AD), some studies show that the activation of the Wnt pathway inhibits the gene expression of the β-secretase gene (BACE1), a key precursor of amyloidβ [7].

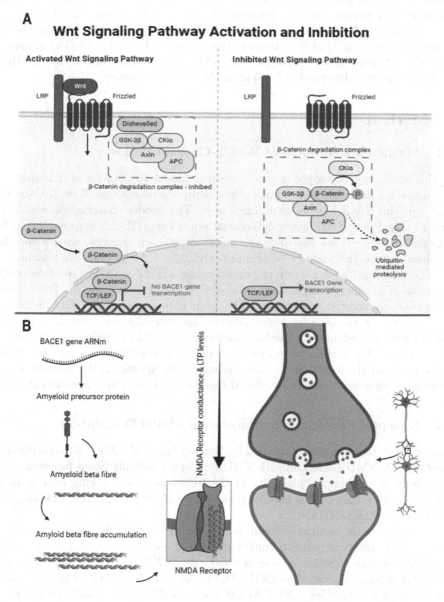

Fig. 1. Mechanisms of activation and inhibition of the Wnt/β-Catenin pathway and its effect on the inhibition of BACE1 expression in AD (A). Mechanism in AD due to accumulation of Amyeloidβ in NMDA receptors and its implication in LTP levels.

In this sense, the Wnt Pathway influences amyloidβ levels. Various mechanisms related to AD are associated with the accumulation of amyloidβ, which could impact the efficiency of synaptic receptors NMDA and AMPA, influencing Long-Term Potentiation (LTP). LTP is a complex process considered as a mechanism that leads to the storage of some types of memories, such as explicit memory. This phenomenon has been studied in different types of synapses, with those in the hippocampus being among the most explored (see Fig. 1B).

This study delves into the nexus of these elements, aiming to computationally model the impact of Wnt/β-Catenin pathway modulation on CA3-CA1 synaptic plasticity. It provides a general understanding of the molecular intricacies that underlie synaptic dysfunction by Wnt in Alzheimer's disease.

2   Methods

2.1   Mathematical Model of Wnt/β-Catenin Pathway

In this study, we developed a mathematical model to depict the dynamics of the signaling pathway, incorporating key components such as Wnt, β-Catenin, GSK3-β, the BACE1 gene, and Amyloid-β. The model construction was executed using Python. Ordinary differential equations (ODEs) were employed to articulate the synthesis and degradation rates of each element, with a specific emphasis on the influence of β-Catenin activity on BACE1 gene expression.

The role of β-Catenin was represented using a Hill function to recreate cooperativity in binding to regulatory sites of BACE1 gene expression. To validate the model, parameters were adjusted to align with experimental data. Sensitivity analyses, cross-validation, and quantitative comparisons were subsequently carried out to evaluate the model's capacity to faithfully reflect experimental observations. These steps were taken to ensure a biologically meaningful interpretation, and the model underwent iterative refinements until achieving a satisfactory agreement between simulated results and observed experimental data.

2.2   Synaptic Plasticity Computational Model Description

The computational model developed by Dainauskas et al. (2023) [8] incorporates the GluN2A-NMDA and GluN2B-NMDA receptor subunit-based functions and their impact on synaptic plasticity in CA3-CA1 synapses, taking into account the assumption that LTP is mainly governed by GluN2B-NMDAR subunit, and LTD by GluN2A-NMDAR.

The schematic diagram shown in Fig. 2 delineates the key elements of the synaptic plasticity model. Initiated by a presynaptic action potential, the NMDAR activates, which are composed of GluN2A-NMDAR and GluN2B-NMDAR subunits, denoted as gNMDAGluN2A and gNMDAGluN2B. This activation induces variables ϕNMDALTP and ϕNMDALTD, which respectively account for the contributions of long-term potentiation (LTP) and long-term depression (LTD).

Upon activation, the LTP variable ϕNMDALTP exerts inhibitory control over the LTD variable ϕNMDALTD, preventing the occurrence of LTD, and viceversa. The postsynaptic local membrane potential V undergoes a low-pass filtering process, resulting in LTP and LTD variables denoted as VLTP and VLTD, respectively. These variables are subsequently multiplied by their corresponding NMDAR-dependent counterparts, ϕNMDALTP and ϕNMDALTD, to generate the LTP and LTD components of the synaptic weight denoted as wAMPR. In this study we integrate into the model the presence of Aß, these levels will be modulated by Wnt pathway (Fig 2 circle in orange), according to literature, Aß could impaired gNMDARGluN2B conductance and resulting in deficits in LTP [5].

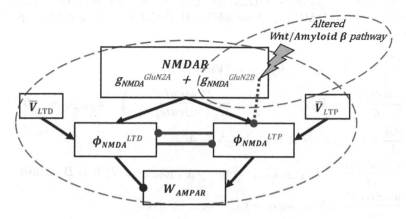

Fig. 2. Key Elements and interaction of the Synaptic Plasticity Model and Wnt/ß-Catenin Pathway. Figure adapted from [8]

This computational model will help us gain insights on how Wnt levels may affect GluN2B-NMDAR function and explore if there is a critical threshold on the interaction between Wnt and Amyeloid-β/Glun2B-NMDAR that leads to the impairment on synaptic plasticity at hippocampal CA1-CA3 synapses.

2.3 Modulation of Wnt/β-Catenin Pathway Levels

To evaluate the pathway within the implemented model, we rely on the function described by the model's authors , specifically the LTP function ϕNMDALTP (t). This function is triggered by gNMDALT P (t), primarily dependent on Glu2BNMDAR synaptic conductance function XgNMDAGlu2NB (t), assuming Glu2NB-NMDAR mediates LTP. The LTP function has a higher Hill coefficient compared to the LTD function. Changes in the time constant values of the LTP function ϕNMDAGLU2NBLTP (t) can regulate receptor impedance values, thereby influencing the synaptic process. This value represents the effect of Aβ in the model. Furthermore, modifications to the Aβ variable values are determined by the activation or deactivation of the Wnt trigger. Based on in vitro reports suggesting variations in levels from 10 nM to 20 nM with effects on Aβ inhibition percentages of 41% and 52%, respectively [9].

3   Results

Wnt/β-Catenin Pathway Model Equations and Validation: To capture the intricate dynamics of the Wnt/β-Catenin signaling pathway, a set of Ordinary Differential Equations (ODEs) was implemented for each key element preselected; Wnt (1), BACE(2), AmyeloidB (3), β-Catenin (4) and GSK3-β (5). The equations are as follows:

1. $\dfrac{dWnt}{dt} = k_{\text{syn\_Wnt}} - k_{\text{deg\_Wnt}} \cdot Wnt$

2. $\dfrac{dBACE1}{dt} = k_{\text{syn\_BACE1}} \left(1 - \dfrac{Bcatenin^n}{K_d^n + Bcatenin^n} \right) - k_{\text{deg\_BACE1}} \cdot BACE1$

3. $\dfrac{dA}{dt} = k_{\text{syn\_AB}} \cdot BACE1 - k_{\text{deg\_AB}} \cdot A$

4. $\dfrac{dBcatenin}{dt} = k_{\text{syn\_Bcatenin}} \cdot Wnt - k_{\text{deg\_Bcatenin}} \cdot GSK3 \cdot Bcatenin$

5. $\dfrac{dGSK3B}{dt} = k_{\text{syn\_GSK3B}} - k_{\text{deg\_GSK3B}} \cdot GSK3$

These equations describe the rate of change for each component within the pathway, considering synthesis, degradation, and regulatory interactions.

Subsequently, the model underwent validation using data from experimental studies to properly calibrate its parameters. The values for various parameters were fine-tuned based on experimental observations. Figure 3B illustrates the dynamic of the model under a basal concentration of Wnt at 50 ng/ml. Additional conditions were explored, including negative regulation with Wnt values at 1 ng/ml (Fig. 3A) and positive regulation with 100 ng/ml (Fig. 3C).

```
1
2    import numpy as np
3    from scipy.integrate import odeint
4    import matplotlib.pyplot as plt
5
6    # Definition of differential equations
7    def model(y, t, k_syn_Wnt, k_deg_Wnt, k_syn_BACE1, k_deg_BACE1, k_syn_A, k_deg_A, n, K_d,
8    k_syn_Bcatenin, k_deg_Bcatenin, k_syn_GSK3, k_deg_GSK3):
9        Wnt, BACE1, A, Bcatenin, GSK3 = y
10
11       dWnt_dt = k_syn_Wnt - k_deg_Wnt * Wnt
12       #BACE1_gen_expression
13       dBACE1_dt = k_syn_BACE1 * (1 - (Bcatenin**n) / (K_d**n + Bcatenin**n)) - k_deg_BACE1 * BACE1
14       # Amyeloid_B_Production
15       dA_dt = k_syn_A * BACE1 - k_deg_A * A
16       dBcatenin_dt = k_syn_Bcatenin * Wnt - k_deg_Bcatenin * GSK3 * Bcatenin
17       dGSK3_dt = k_syn_GSK3 - k_deg_GSK3 * GSK3
18
19       return [dWnt_dt, dBACE1_dt, dA_dt, dBcatenin_dt, dGSK3_dt]
20
21   # Model parameters
22   k_syn_Wnt = 0.05
23   k_deg_Wnt = 0.05
24   k_syn_BACE1 = 1.5
25   k_deg_BACE1 = 0.1
26   k_syn_A = 0.09
27   k_deg_A = 0.1
28   n = 2  #Hill Coefficient
29   K_d = 10  # Disociation constant
30   k_syn_Bcatenin = 0.1
31   k_deg_Bcatenin = 0.05
32   k_syn_GSK3 = 0.1
33   k_deg_GSK3 = 0.09
34
35   # Initial conditions
36   y0 = [0, 0, 0, 0, 0]
37
38   # Simulation time
39   time = np.linspace(0, 100, 1000)
40
41   #Solution of differential equations
42
43   solution = odeint(model, y0, time, args=(k_syn_Wnt, k_deg_Wnt, k_syn_BACE1, k_deg_BACE1, k_syn_A,
44   k_deg_A, n, K_d, k_syn_Bcatenin, k_deg_Bcatenin, k_syn_GSK3, k_deg_GSK3))
45
46   # Viewing the results
47   plt.figure(figsize=(10, 6))
48   #plt.plot(time, solution[:, 0], label='Wnt')
49   plt.plot(time, solution[:, 0], label='Wnt: {:.2f} ng/ml'.format(solucion[-1, 0]))
50   plt.plot(time, solution[:, 3], label='-Catenin')
51   plt.plot(time, solution[:, 4], label='GSK3')
52   plt.plot(time, solution[:, 1], label='BACE1')
53   plt.plot(time, solution[:, 2], label='Amyeloid')
54   plt.title('Dynamics of the Wnt/-Catenin pathway')
55   plt.xlabel('Time')
56   plt.ylabel('Levels')
57   plt.legend()
58   plt.show()
59
```

For the equation implementation we use Python and the code can be seen above, were we define some parameters such as (k_syn) and (k_deg) that refer to the synthesis and degradation rate for each element in the pathway. All of these rates were adjusted based in experimental data. Specifically the dynamic of the model response to k_syn_Wnt parameter variation, the values of 0,05 and 5 recreate a 1 ng/ml and 100 ng/ml of Wnt respectably at the final time of simulation.

Also we included (n) as the Hill coefficient and (k_d) as the coefficient of dissociation. The Hill coefficient describes the cooperativity in the binding of the ligand to the receptor, while the dissociation coefficient describes the affinity between the ligand and the receptor. Both are important for understanding how ligands interact with their receptors in biological systems. In these case the interaction between the proteins for activate or deactivate its function.

For the validation of the Wnt pathway mathematical model, we analyze each element individually to determine its response compared to experimental in vitro reports. In the case of the influence of Wnt levels modulation on β-Catenin protein levels, we compare with experimental data where reports indicating that an increase in Wnt protein levels increases β-Catenin levels in an a linear way. In concentrations of rWnt-3A, the intensity of quantitative western blot analysis showed values of 0.12 for control condition, 0.17 for 100 ng/ml and 0.23 for 200 ng/ml condition. In our model, we replicate this within the range of 1 to 100 ng/ml (Fig. 4A) [10]. On the other hand, for GSK3-β protein, we conduct a similar analysis and find that experimental reports showed that the exposition of 20 ng/ml of Wnt levels from 0 240 min do not significantly impact GSK3-β levels. In our model, we observe that variations in Wnt levels from 0 to 90 ng/ml result in fluctuations in GSK3-β levels from 9.0 to 9.6 and finally a decrease to 8 at 100 ng/ml (Fig. 4C) [11]. Regarding the BACE1 gene and Amyloid-β protein, experimental conditions with 20 nm/ml of Wnt decrease BACE1 gene expression in ≈ 60% and protein syntesis in ≈ 25% (Fig. 4B) [9]. Finally, in exploring the effects of Amyloid-β on the conductance of NMDA receptors, we find reports indicating that treatment with these molecule negatively impacts excitatory postsynaptic potential (EPSP), correlating with alterations in conductance and a decrease in the gene expression of NMDA receptor precursors (Fig. 4D) [12].

Receptor Conductance Variation: The Wnt pathway modulation and the synaptic plasticity model response to different Wnt concentrations to manifest in altered N-methyl-D-aspartate receptor (NMDAR) impedance values. This change in receptor impedance responds to Amyeloid-β concentration values, which modify the conductance values of the Glu2B subunit of the NMDA receptor in the variable Alpha nr2b of the authors' model (Table 1). In this sense the Wnt and synaptic model connection recreate the regulatory effect of Wnt on the synaptic process, reflecting the modulation of calcium influx and downstream signaling pathways.

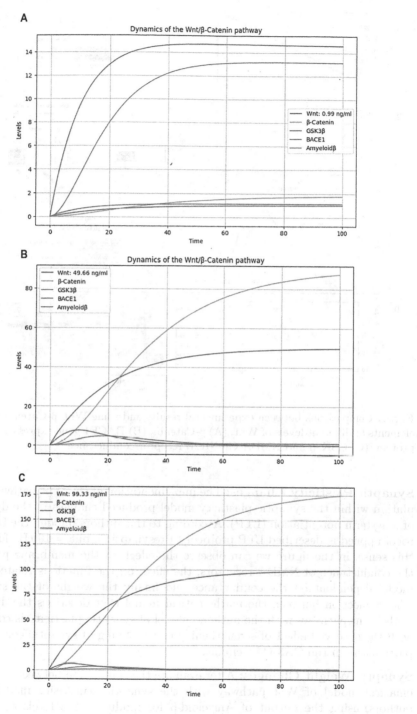

Fig. 3. Dynamics of the Wnt/ß-Catenin pathway at different levels of Wnt, (A) Wnt at 1 ng/mL, (B) Wnt at 50 ng/mL and (C) Wnt at 100 ng/mL

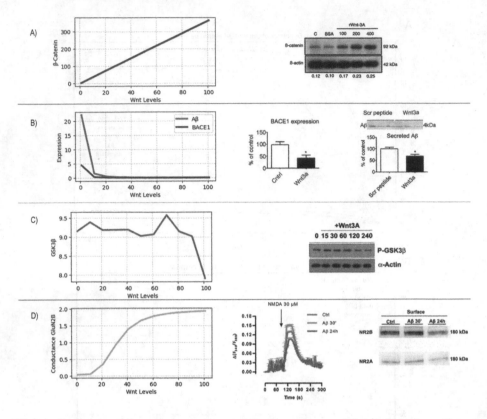

Fig. 4. Comparisons between experimental results and some Wnt/β-Catenin pathway elements at different levels of Wnt, (A) β-Catenin, (B) BACE1 gene expression and Aβ protein, (C) GSK3β and NMDA GluNR2B receptor conductance

Synaptic Plasticity Changes: The implementation of the Wnt pathway modulation within the synaptic plasticity model produced changes in the dynamics of long-term potentiation (LTP). According to the authors' model, the LTP protocol applied is described LTP protocol - Presynaptic input = 100 Hz for 1 s. In this sense, in the figure we can observe the effect on the membrane potential, the conductance of NMDA receptors, the effect on the functions related in the model dependent on the conductance and finally the weight of the synapses. The connection between the mathematical model that describes the dynamics of the Wnt pathway with the authors' model of synaptic plasticity is consistent with the observed effect of strengthening or weakening of synaptic connections, particularly in the CA3-CA1 circuit.

Synaptic Weight Changes: After evaluate the connection between our mathematical model of Wnt pathway with the synaptic palastisity model of the authors, using the output of Amyeloid-β for modulate the levels of NMDA-GluN2B conductance levels (Alpha nr2b parameter in synaptic model) we

Table 1. Dynamics at different levels of Wnt for each element of the molecular pathway and its influence on GluN2b subunit NMDA receptor conductance

Wnt	GSK3-B	B-Catenin	BACE1-Gen	AmyeloidB	Conductance-GluN2B
0	1.11	0	14.99	13.49	0.04
10.13	1.11	17.8	3.73	3.58	0.27
20.26	1.1	35.6	1.15	1.14	1.14
30.39	1.1	53.4	0.54	0.54	1.62
40.52	1.09	71.2	0.31	0.32	1.77
50.65	1.09	89	0.2	0.21	1.83
60.78	1.09	106.81	0.14	0.15	1.85
70.91	1.09	124.61	0.1	0.11	1.86
81.05	1.08	142.41	0.08	0.09	1.87
91.18	1.08	160.21	0.06	0.07	1.88
101.13	1.07	178.01	0.05	0.06	1.88

proceed to modulate the Wnt levels on the synaptic plasticisy model. The authors evaluate the synaptic plasticity in different ways for example in the contexct of Frequency-Dependent LTP protocol using a graphic output (Fig. 5) that evidences the effects over membrane potential, NMDA receptor conducatances, NMDA dependent funtions that we describe previously in the methods section and the synaptic weight, given that experimental evidences suggest that Wnt pathway is related with Alzhaymer disease mainly in the context of inlfuence the LTP proccess of synapses, we focus in this scene for evaluate our Wnt modulation influence. How we can see at Fig. 5; the membrane potential, NMDA receptor conductances, NMDA dependent funtions and the synaptic weight, a critical parameter in synaptic plasticity, was influenced by the varying levels (1 Fig. (5A), 10 (5B), 15 (5C), 20 (5D) and 49 (5E) ng/ml of WNT). This reflects the model's ability to replicate the reported in vitro findings where WNT levels impact the percentage of amyloidβ (Aβ) inhibition, and consequently affects the conduction of NMDA receptors, the weight of the synapse is altered. The dynamics of the model in the Wnt ranges from 1 to 40 (ng/ml) showed a modulatory effect that is evident in the gradual increase in the weight of the synapse, from 50 to 100 (ng/ml) the effects are less evident, suggesting a saturation effect on the dynamics of the model. In the sense that the conductance values in the authors' model varied in range between 0.02 and 1.9 in the case of our mathematical model and the connection with conductance values in the function for Glu2B in the variable Alpha nr2b, as We observe in Table 1, values at 0 of Wnt show 0.024, while in the case of 10, 30, 50 and 100 the values are 0.27, 1.62, 1.85 and 1.88 respectively.

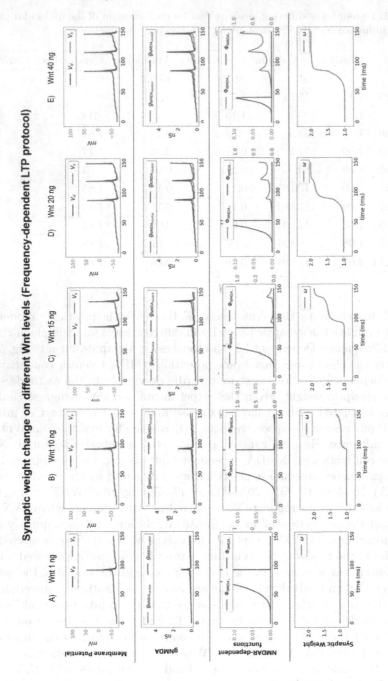

Fig. 5. Wnt modulation effects on membrane potential, NMDA receptor subunits conductances, NMDA receptor functions and Synaptic weight in final row. Each colummn in graph represent different Wnt concentration level starting from left to right A,B,C,D,E (1, 10, 15, 20 y 40) ng/ml. Figure adapted from [8]

4   Discussion

The results obtained in this study provide a comprehensive understanding of the Wnt/β-Catenin pathway impact on synaptic plasticity and its potential role in Alzheimer's disease (AD). The combination of computational modeling and experimental validation enhances our grasp of the complex dynamics involved in these intricate molecular processes. The set of Ordinary Differential Equations (ODEs) employed to model the Wnt/β-Catenin pathway recreate the synthesis, degradation, and regulatory interactions of key elements such as Wnt, BACE1, Amyloid-β, β-Catenin, and GSK3-β. The model underwent validation with experimental data, with parameters fine-tuned to align with observed data (Fig. 3).

The study successfully explored the modulation of the Wnt pathway and its consequential effects on synaptic plasticity. Changes in N-methyl-D-aspartate receptor (NMDAR) demonstrated the impact of Wnt concentrations on the conductance of the GluN2B subunit, reflecting the intricate relationship between the Wnt pathway and synaptic processes. Integration of the Wnt pathway modulation within the synaptic plasticity model revealed notable alterations in long-term potentiation (LTP) dynamics. The observed effects on membrane potential, NMDA receptor conductance, and synaptic weight align with experimental findings. The variation in synaptic weight, a critical parameter in synaptic plasticity, showcased a modulatory effect of Wnt levels.

A recent publication [13] by the synaptic model authors explores the influence of specific AD peptides on synaptic plasticity, our research delves into the intricate interactions between the Wnt pathway and synaptic plasticity in the Alzheimer's context. Together, these studies provide a comprehensive understanding of the molecular and synaptic processes involved in AD, offering a holistic perspective for future investigations and potential therapeutic approaches. The integration of findings from both studies contributes to a more nuanced comprehension of the multifaceted mechanisms underlying Alzheimer's disease. While our study provides valuable insights, it is not without limitations. The computational model simplifies the intricate biological reality, and further refinements can enhance its accuracy. Additionally, the in vitro conditions may not perfectly replicate the complexities of the in vivo environment, emphasizing the need for cautious interpretation of the results.

5   Conclusion

In conclusion, the integration of a validated computational model of the Wnt/β-Catenin pathway with synaptic plasticity provides a nuanced understanding of their interplay and implications for AD. The observed modulatory effects on synaptic weight and NMDA receptor conductance underscore the multi-mechanistic nature of Wnt pathway involvement in neurodegenerative processes. This study lays the foundation for future investigations aiming to unravel the complexities of these intricate molecular interactions, offering potential avenues for therapeutic interventions in AD.

Acknowledgment. This work started as a students project during the IX Latin American School on Computational Neuroscience (LASCON 2024), held in São Paulo, Brazil, January 8 - February 2, 2024, and supported by FAPESP (grant 2023/06880-4), CNPq (grant 445851/2023-6) and the IBRO-LARC Schools Funding Program.

References

1. Fan, X., Markram, H.: A brief history of simulation neuroscience. Front. Neuroinform. **13**, 32 (2019)
2. Brigman, J.L., et al.: Loss of GluN2B-containing NMDA receptors in CA1 hippocampus and cortex impairs long-term depression, reduces dendritic spine density, and disrupts learning. J. Neurosci. **30**(13), 4590–4600 (2010)
3. Dalton, G.L., Wu, D.C., Wang, Y.T., Floresco, S.B., Phillips, A.G.: NMDA GluN2A and GluN2B receptors play separate roles in the induction of LTP and ltd in the amygdala and in the acquisition and extinction of conditioned fear. Neuropharmacology **62**(2), 797–806 (2012)
4. Liu, J., Chang, L., Song, Y., Li, H., Wu, Y.: The role of NMDA receptors in Alzheimer's disease. Front. Neurosci. **13**, 43 (2019)
5. Taniguchi, K., et al.: Amyloid-β oligomers interact with NMDA receptors containing GluN2A subunits and metabotropic glutamate receptor 1 in primary cortical neurons: relevance to the synapse pathology of Alzheimer's disease. Neurosci. Res. **180**, 90–98 (2022)
6. Jia, L., Piña-Crespo, J., Li, Y.: Restoring Wnt/β-catenin signaling is a promising therapeutic strategy for Alzheimer's disease. Mol. Brain **12**, 1–11 (2019)
7. MacDonald, B.T., Tamai, K., He, X.: Wnt/β-catenin signaling: components, echanisms, and diseases. Dev. Cell **17**(1), 9–26 (2009)
8. Dainauskas, J.J., Marie, H., Migliore, M., Saudargiene, A.: GluN2B-NMDAR subunit contribution on synaptic plasticity: a phenomenological model for CA3-CA1 synapses. Front. Synaptic Neurosci. **15**, 1113957 (2023)
9. Parr, C., Mirzaei, N., Christian, M., Sastre, M.: Activation of the Wnt/β-catenin pathway represses the transcription of the β-amyloid precursor protein cleaving enzyme (bace1) via binding of t-cell factor-4 to bace1 promoter. FASEB J. **29**(2), 623–635 (2015)
10. Chuang, K., et al.: Evaluation of anti-Wnt/β-catenin signaling agents by pGL4-top transfected stable cells with a luciferase eporter system. Braz. J. Med. Biol. Res. **43**(10), 931–941 (2010). https://doi.org/10.1590/s0100-879x2010007500091
11. Kim, J.-G., et al.: Wnt3A induces GSK-3β phosphorylation and β-catenin accumulation through RhoA/ROCK. J. Cell. Physiol. **232**(5), 1104–1113 (2017)
12. Ortiz-Sanz, C., et al.: Amyloid β/PKC-dependent alterations in NMDA receptor composition are detected in early stages of Alzheimer's disease. Cell Death Dis. **13**(3), 253 (2022). https://doi.org/10.1038/s41419-022-04687-y
13. Dainauskas, J.J., Vitale, P., Moreno, S., Marie, H., Migliore, M., Saudargiene, A.: Altered synaptic plasticity at hippocampal CA1–CA3 synapses in Alzheimer's disease: integration of amyloid precursor protein intracellular domain and amyloid beta effects into computational models. Front. Comput. Neurosci. **17** (2023)

In Silico Application of the Epsilon-Greedy Algorithm for Frequency Optimization of Electrical Neurostimulation for Hypersynchronous Disorders

Gabriel da Silva Lima[1,3] ⓘ, Vinícius Rosa Cota[2](✉) ⓘ,
and Wallace Moreira Bessa[3] ⓘ

[1] RoboTeAM - Robotics and Machine Learning, Universidade Federal do Rio Grande do Norte, Natal, Brazil
[2] Rehab Technologies Lab, Istituto Italiano di Tecnologia, Genova, Italy
vinicius.rosacota@iit.it
[3] Faculty of Technology, University of Turku, Turku, Finland
{gdasil,wmobes}@utu.fi

Abstract. One of the most promising alternatives to suppress epileptic seizures in drug-resistant and neurosurgery-refractory patients is using electro-electronic devices. By applying an appropriate pulsatile electrical stimulation, the process of ictogenesis can be quickly suppressed. However, in designing such stimulation devices, a common problem is defining suitable parameters such as pulse amplitude, duration, and frequency. In this work, we propose a machine learning technique based on the epsilon-greedy algorithm to optimize the pulse frequency which could prevent abnormal neuronal activity without exceeding energy usage for the stimulation. Five different simulations were carried out in order to evaluate the contribution of the energy consumption in determining the minimum frequency. The results show the efficacy of the proposed algorithm to search the minimum pulse frequency necessary to suppress epileptic seizures.

Keywords: Epilepsy · Seizure suppression · Machine Learning · Epsilon-greedy · Optimization

1 Introduction

Neuropathologies such as epilepsy, motor disorders, neuropsychiatric dysfunctions, and many others still represent a major cause of adult-onset disability worldwide [5]. This has a profoundly negative impact on the lives of patients, families, communities, and in the society as whole, displaying a muti-faceted impairment of aspects that range from the quality of life of individuals to the economic health of nations (particularly those of aging populations). Furthermore, first choice treatments such as pharmacotherapy, neurosurgery, or physical therapy often fall short of delivering full relief of symptoms or robust recovery of neural function. For instance, in epilepsy, circa 30% of the patients do not obtain full control of seizures with anti-epileptic drugs, and, among these, half can not be submitted to curative ablative neurosurgery [9,17]. Considering the great prevalence of the disease worldwide (1 - 2% of the world population), these numbers represent millions of individuals suffering from uncontrollable seizures [7,16].

A promising alternative is the use of technology to interface the brain with electro-electronic devices in the pursuit of controlling and/or rectifying aberrant brain activity which may provide treatment of symptoms or even full recovery and cure. Broadly termed neurotechnologies, such an approach consists both of reading descriptive signals from the brain and of controlling the activity of neuronal cells by means of directly applying stimuli of different physical forms, bypassing somatosensory neural functions. Among many possibilities, electrophysiological interfaces are the most well developed and broadly used in both experimental and clinical scenarios. In fact, electrophysiological recordings (such as the electroencephalogram, electrocorticogram, local field potentials, and multi-unit recordings) and electrical stimulation of the nervous systems (Deep Brain Stimulation (DBS), Vagus Nerve Stimulation (VNS), transcranial Electrical Stimulation (tES), etc.) have served not only as powerful diagnostic tools, but also as effective alternatives to pharmacoresistant neurological scenarios [1,2,8,10,12].

From the start of its modern age in the sixties, neurotechnology in general and electrical stimulation in particular have seen great progress due to important advances in neuroscientific knowledge, neurosurgery, and digital technology [6]. More recently, unprecedented technological breakthrough such as disruptive neuronal sensor technology, very-large scale integration of electronic circuits, machine learning techniques, neuromorphism, and other breakthroughs are spurring yet another major paradigm shift in the field: close-loop approaches [3,4]. In reality, the vast majority of clinical or experimental applications, neurotechnology is still used in an open-loop fashion only, in which neural stimulation is delivered with a fixed set of parameters, changing only in the case of the intervention of the expert. In this case, electrophysiological recordings are used only prior to stimulation as a means of diagnosis or after treatment to assess therapeutic efficacy of neuromodulation. Conversely, closed-loop neuroengineering systems, in which stimulation is directly controlled in real time by features of electrophysiological recordings, have been shown to be superior as it can dynamically respond to the highly non-stationary nature of brain activity to find privileged windows for delivering stimulus and to fine-tune its parameters. This, in turn, provides increased efficacy (stronger therapeutic effect) and efficiency (stimulation delivered only when needed).

Naturally, to be able to close the loop, one must design computational/mathematical strategies capable of connecting in real time features of the electrophysiological recordings to the parameters of electrical stimulation. Preferentially, this should be done in a way to optimize hardware resources while decreasing the risk of the therapy. For instance, in a closed-loop system to treat epilepsy, once detected, seizures must be suppressed as fast as possible by using the minimum amount of energy in the stimulation protocol, which can be translated to reduced pulse frequency, amplitude, and duration in a conventional pulsatile electrical stimulation.

In this work, we used a network of Izhikevich neurons which undergoes gradual increases of synaptic weights to simulate an ictogenesis process (development of a seizure) in a computational testbed. Local field potentials were computed to detect aberrant patterns of neural activity and electrical stimulation was applied to control it. Closing the loop, an ε-greedy algorithm was applied to quickly suppress seizures as quickly as possible, while searching for the minimum frequency of stimulation.

2   Neuronal Model

The nonlinear integrate-and-fire model introduced by Izhikevich captures the diverse firing patterns observed in real biological neurons [11,14] efficiently. This renders the model biophysically plausible, making it highly suitable for conducting large-scale simulations. The model can be represented by the following set of equations:

$$\dot{v} = 0.04 D_v v + 5v + 140 - u + I + J \tag{1}$$

$$\dot{u} = D_a(D_b v - u) \tag{2}$$

$$\text{if } v_k \geq 30 \text{ mV, then } \begin{cases} v_k \leftarrow c_k \\ u_k \leftarrow u_k + d_k \end{cases} \tag{3}$$

which v represents the membrane potential of the neuron, u stands for a membrane recovery variable, D_x is the diagonal matrix of x, I denotes the synaptic currents, J the inject current, and a, b, c, and d being dimensionless parameters.

Considering that the model (1) represents a network of N_e excitatory neurons and N_i inhibitory, the Euler method with time steps of 0.02 ms was employed to simulate a neuronal population with $N_e = 800$ and $N_i = 200$. The network is full-connected by the matrix of synaptic weights $S \in \mathbb{R}^{N \times N}$, where each s_{mn} weight is obtained from a continuous uniform distribution with amplitude 0.1 for the excitatory neurons and -0.1 for the inhibitory.

This work considered the initial states of v and u as being $v_0 = -70 + 10r$ mV and $u_0 = -15 + 3r$ mV, with r standing for a N-dimensional vector of random numbers extracted from a continuous uniform distribution between 0 and 1, with $N = N_e + N_i$. The dimensionless parameters are defined as follows:

$$\begin{aligned} D_{a,k} &= 0.02 \\ D_{b,k} &= 0.3 \\ c_k &= -65 - 13r_e \\ d_k &= 8 + 0.8r_e \end{aligned} \qquad 1 \leq k \leq N_e$$

$$\begin{aligned} D_{a,k} &= 0.02 + 4 \times 10^{-4} r_i \\ D_{b,k} &= 0.3 - 0.06 r_i \\ c_k &= -65 \\ d_k &= 8 \end{aligned} \qquad N_e + 1 \leq k \leq N$$

with r_e and r_i being random numbers extracted from a continuous uniform distribution between 0 and 1. The synaptic current I can be modeled by the sum of the fired neuron currents with the background current which represents the unmodeled electrical activity of the brain:

$$I = I_f + I_b \tag{4}$$

where $I_{f,k} = \sum_m s_{k,m}$, which $s_{k,m}$ represents the synaptic weight from the f-fired neuron connected to the k-neuron. The background current I_b is given by a normal distribution with null mean and variance of 4 for the excitatory neurons and 36 for the inhibitory.

The Fig. 1 shows the raster plot and the local field potential (LFP) of the neuronal model simulated as described above. The inject current was set to be null. The LFP was calculated by the weighted average of v with weights obtained from a continuous uniform distribution.

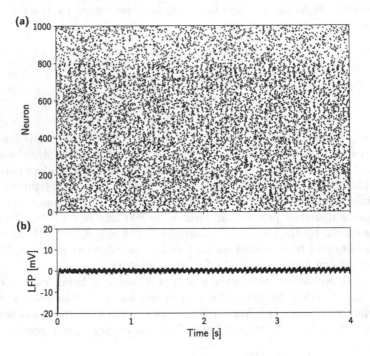

Fig. 1. Simulation with normal network activity: (a) raster plot and (b) LFP signal.

2.1   Induction of Ictogenesis

The process of ictogenesis was simulated by a gradual increment of the synaptic weights from 0.1 and -0.1 to 2 and -4 corresponding to the excitatory and inhibitory neurons, respectively. The results are shown in the Fig. 2.

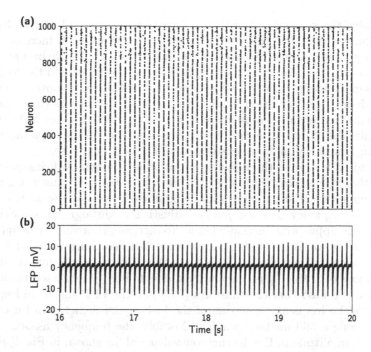

Fig. 2. Network synchronization by modification in synaptic weights: (a) raster plot and (b) LFP signal.

In order to suppress this aberrant activity, a train of pulses of electrical current J_k should be applied as follows:

$$J_k = \nu_k \bar{J} \max\{0, \text{sgn}[\cos(2\pi t f) - \cos(\pi d f)]\} \tag{5}$$

where ν_k is the weight, obtained by an uniform distribution, that relates the train of amplitude $\bar{J}$ to the k-neuron, d is the pulse duration, f the frequency of pulses, and $\text{sgn}(x)$ is the standard relay function. The objective here is to search the optimum frequency f given $\bar{J} = 200\ \mu A$ and $d = 0.1$ ms.

3 The ε-Greedy Algorithm

The ε-greedy is a reinforcement learning algorithm designed to solve the multi-armed bandit (MAB) problem [18]. The problem of MAB was introduced by [15], and it consists of an agent who is presented with a range of actions, commonly known as "arms", where each action generates a specific reward upon selection. The primary goal of the agent is to optimize its total accumulated reward throughout a sequence of engagements. It achieves this by acquiring an understanding of which actions are more advantageous and leveraging this knowledge to enhance its decision-making abilities as time progresses.

Basically, the ε-greedy algorithm is based on the control of the degree of exploration by changing the parameter ε. If the value of ε increases (more exploratory), the average reward will be initially low but will become higher as the agent discovers and explores the best actions. However, in the long term, due to its exploratory nature, the agent might not stick to the optimal action as much as desired. On the other hand, if the value of ε decreases (more exploitative), the average reward will increase more slowly, but this is the right strategy to maximize the expected reward in the next step. Unlike the exploratory case, in the long run, it will more frequently choose the optimal case.

Our objective here is the desynchronization of the neuron firing pattern by the injection of electrical current in the form of a train of pulses. Given that both the amplitude and pulse duration remain fixed, the variable we will manipulate is the frequency of these pulses, adjusting it through an algorithm. To determine the appropriate action-whether to increase, decrease, or maintain the pulse frequency-we must establish a criterion for discerning aberrant behavior within the neuronal population. To achieve this, our approach involves utilizing the frequency with the highest magnitude, denoted as f_a, obtained through the application of a Fast Fourier Transform (FFT) on the LFP signal. In Fig. 3, you can observe the frequency spectrum of the LFP signal depicted in Figs. 1b and 2b, considering a 300 ms time window. Notably, the frequency associated with the highest amplitude in the desynchronized signal, as shown in Fig. 1, exhibits a greater magnitude than that of the synchronized LFP signal.

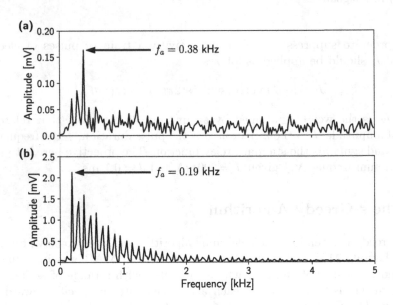

Fig. 3. Frequency spectrum for the LFP signal: (a) presented at the Fig. 1b and (b) presented at the Fig. 2b.

The Algorithm 1 provides a concise summary of the steps involved in the ε-greedy scheme. It is worth noting that the actions taken within this scheme are directly linked to the adjustment of pulse frequency, either increasing or decreasing it by 10 Hz. This decision carries significance as higher frequencies not only induce desynchronization in neuron firing but also result in an increase in energy consumption associated with the external stimulus. To address this dual concern, the reward function is designed to take into account both the current state variable and the pulse frequency itself, aiming to identify a frequency that not only promotes desynchronization but also minimizes the overall energy expenditure of the stimulus. The reward function is defined as follows:

$$r = 0.01[10\exp(5|\vartheta - \vartheta_{max}|/\vartheta_{max}) + p_s \exp(5f/f_{max}) - 40] \qquad (6)$$

with $\vartheta_{max} = 4$ representing the maximum attainable state variable, while f_{max} denotes the expected maximum frequency. Additionally, the parameter p_s plays a pivotal role, representing the weight of the pulse frequency in determining its optimal value without exceeding the total energy of the external stimulus.

Algorithm 1. ε-greedy algorithm.

Set exploration probability ε
Initialize main reward $\bar{R} \leftarrow 0$
Initialize specific reward $R(a) \leftarrow 0$, for a from 1 to k
loop
    Pick a random number p between 0 and 1
    if $p < \varepsilon$ **then**
        Choose an action randomly
        $A \leftarrow \text{random}(a)$
    else
        Choose the action that minimizes $R(a)$
        $A \leftarrow \arg\min_a R(a)$
    end if
    Apply A into the model and receive the reward r
    According to the previous $\bar{R}$, define the specific reward R_a
    Calculate the main reward: $\bar{R} \leftarrow \bar{R} + \alpha_1(r - \bar{R})$
    Calculate the specific reward: $R(a) \leftarrow R(a) + \alpha_2(R_a - R(a))$
end loop

As mentioned previously, we have established three distinct actions: action 0, which maintains the pulse frequency unchanged; action 1, designed to increase the frequency; and action 2, intended to decrease it. To further incentivize the action that leads to a significant enhancement in the main reward, denoted as $\bar{R}$, and to discourage the other actions, we have defined a set of specific rewards as follows:

$$R_a = \begin{matrix} a=0 \\ \begin{bmatrix} -1 & 0.5 & 0.5 \\ 0.5 & -1 & -1 \end{bmatrix} \end{matrix} \begin{matrix} a=1 \\ \begin{bmatrix} -0.1 & -1 & 0.5 \\ -1 & 0.5 & -1 \end{bmatrix} \end{matrix} \begin{matrix} a=2 \\ \begin{bmatrix} -0.1 & 0.5 & -1 \\ -1 & -1 & 0.5 \end{bmatrix} \end{matrix} \qquad (7)$$

For instance, consider a scenario where the preceding action involved an increase in the parameter f, resulting in a decrease in the primary reward $\bar{R}$. In such cases, we opt for the first row of specific rewards within the central matrix defined in equation (7). This entails assigning values of $R_0 = -0.1$ to action 0, $R_1 = -1$ to action 1, and $R_2 = 0.5$ to action 2. Conversely, if the prior action led to an improvement in $\bar{R}$, the second row of the same matrix is utilized to determine the corresponding rewards. It should be pointed out that Gaussian noise with a variance of 0.1 was added to the reward matrix (7) in order to emulate a stochastic environment and increase the robustness of the algorithm.

4   Simulation Results

The ε-greedy algorithm was employed with time steps set at 400 ms, utilizing parameter values of $\varepsilon = 0.2$, $\alpha_1 = 0.9$, and $\alpha_2 = 0.2$. To comprehensively assess the impact of varying p_s, we conducted 10 distinct simulations for each p_s. As illustrated in Fig. 4, this figure displays the average outcomes alongside their corresponding variances for each p_s. As anticipated, due to the inclusion of pulse frequency within the reward function, in a task aimed at minimization, an increase in the value of p_s corresponds to a reduction in the final frequency. This outcome signifies a lower energy consumption by the electrode.

Concerning the impact on the frequency of highest amplitude in the Fourier spectrum, denoted as f_a, it becomes evident that these effects diminish as the values of p_s increase, as depicted in Fig. 5. However, even with p_s set to 60, we observe a f_a value of 996 Hz, which exceeds the requirement, especially when comparing it to the frequency of highest amplitude in a desynchronous signal, as shown in Fig. 3b, where f_a is at 380 Hz. For the scenario with $p_s = 60$, the mean pulse frequency stabilizes at approximately $f = 159$ Hz in the steady state,

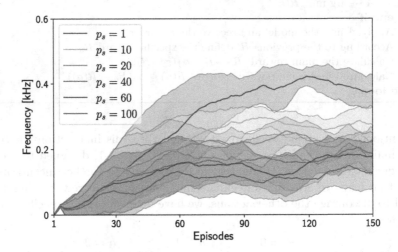

Fig. 4. The p_s parameter.

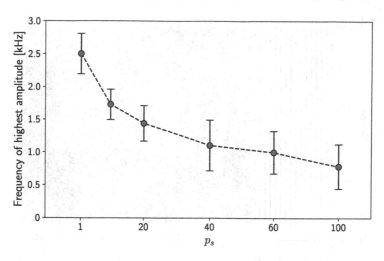

Fig. 5. Simulation results for the ε-greedy algorithm changing the p_s parameter.

as illustrated in Fig. 4. This particular frequency translates to a more efficient energy consumption profile when compared to the higher values of p_s.

The results depicted in Fig. 6 provide a visual representation of the raster plot and LFP generated when the pulse frequency is set to $f = 159$ Hz, as determined by the ε-greedy algorithm. As observed, this choice of pulse frequency achieved the desired desynchronization of the raster plot without necessitating excessive control effort.

4.1   Results Remarks

Some points of the obtained results must be highlighted. The parameter ε is directly related to the algorithm's convergence. While increasing ε, the convergence cannot be guaranteed due to the fact that the agent will choose more random actions; decreasing it will restrict the exploration of other scenarios (frequencies). The chosen value of 0.2 was the best value found to balance the trade-off.

Other important aspects are the limitations of the reductionist computational approach used here. Beginning with the neural tissue model, as an all-to-all connected network with few neurons (1000) of no particular type (dimensionless parameters varied randomly), it does not faithfully reproduce cytoarchitectonics of any circuitry involved in ictogenic phenomena. Furthermore, the simplistic method for the calculation of LFP does not consider specific aspects of neurophysics. Instead, given its tremendous complexity in real life, here we merely used a uniformly randomized weight vector to encompass all possible factors (e.g. cell dimensions, geometry, distance, field conduction pathway, etc.). On the other hand, we do not believe that these issues represent a significant impact on the conclusions here. First, although simple, the network can produce dynamical

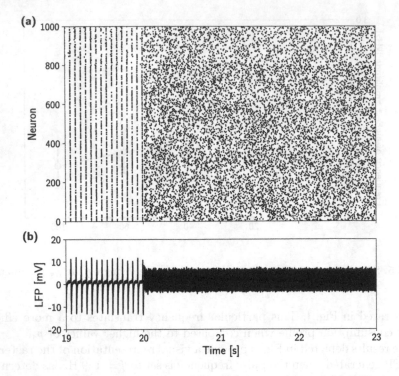

Fig. 6. Simulation results for $f = 159$ Hz: (a) raster plot and (b) LFP signal.

features of interest, particularly stable states related to different levels of synchronization, the transition of which can be induced or modulated (such as in epilepsy) [13]. By its turn, LFP signals were used here only as a tool to detect the state of the network by means of an indirect measurement of biophysical factors, mimicking how it would be done by electrophysiological recordings in real-life closed-loop neurotechnologies. In any case and of course, frequency and time values found in this study must not be taken by their face values. Yet, this was never the intention. Conversely, the main purpose of this work was to assess the feasibility of the investigation of automatic intelligent control strategies using computational neuroscience tools. Experiments with more sophisticated and realistic approaches must be carried out if one wishes to implement such technologies in lab setups or even clinical scenarios.

5   Conclusions

This paper introduces the application of a machine learning algorithm to discover the optimal frequency of a pulse train used to mitigate ictogenesis in a network of neurons. To model the neuronal mass, a mathematical framework based on the work of Izhikevich [11], capable of representing both normal and pathological firing patterns, is employed. To counteract these abnormal neuronal activities, a pulse train is administered. The ε-greedy algorithm is leveraged to determine the pulse frequency required to disrupt synchronous behavior-a hallmark of undesired signals observed in epileptic seizures-while minimizing excessive control effort. The algorithm's effectiveness is assessed through computational simulations, revealing that the ε-greedy approach successfully identifies the essential pulse frequency to suppress the disorder. In any case, given the very straightforward nature of computational methods applied to simulate neural tissue activity here, it is crucial to perform additional experiments with more sophisticated approaches to better understand the feasibility of using automatic intelligent control methods in closed-loop neurotechnologies.

Acknowledgments. This work was supported by the Marie Skłodowska-Curie Individual Fellowship MoRPHEUS granted to VC, Grant Agreement no. 101032054, funded by the European Union under the framework programme H2020-EU.1.3. - EXCELLENT SCIENCE, and by the Brazilian research agencies CNPq and CAPES.

References

1. Alamri, A., Pereira, E.A.: Deep brain stimulation for chronic pain. Neurosurg. Clin. **33**(3), 311–321 (2022)
2. Bao, S.c., Khan, A., Song, R., Tong, R.K.Y.: Rewiring the lesioned brain: electrical stimulation for post-stroke motor restoration. J. stroke **22**(1), 47 (2020)
3. Carè, M., Chiappalone, M., Cota, V.R.: Personalized strategies of neurostimulation: from static biomarkers to dynamic closed-loop assessment of neural function. Front. Neurosci. **18**, 1363128 (2024)
4. Chiappalone, M., et al.: Neuromorphic-based neuroprostheses for brain rewiring: state-of-the-art and perspectives in neuroengineering. Brain Sci. **12**(11), 1578 (2022)
5. Chin, J.H., Vora, N.: The global burden of neurologic diseases. Neurology **83**(4), 349–351 (2014)
6. Cota, V.R., Cançado, S.A.V., Moraes, M.F.D.: On temporal scale-free non-periodic stimulation and its mechanisms as an infinite improbability drive of the brain's functional connectogram. Front. Neuroinform. **17**, 1173597 (2023)
7. Engel, J.: Epilepsy: Global Issues for the Practicing Neurologist, vol. 2. Demos Medical Publishing (2005)
8. Figee, M., Riva-Posse, P., Choi, K.S., Bederson, L., Mayberg, H.S., Kopell, B.H.: Deep brain stimulation for depression. Neurotherapeutics **19**(4), 1229–1245 (2022)
9. French, J.A.: Refractory epilepsy: clinical overview. Epilepsia **48**, 3–7 (2007)
10. Hariz, M., Blomstedt, P.: Deep brain stimulation for parkinson's disease. J. Intern. Med. **292**(5), 764–778 (2022)
11. Izhikevich, E.M.: Simple model of spiking neurons. IEEE Trans. Neural Netw. **14**(6), 1569–1572 (2003)
12. Laxpati, N.G., Kasoff, W.S., Gross, R.E.: Deep brain stimulation for the treatment of epilepsy: circuits, targets, and trials. Neurotherapeutics **11**, 508–526 (2014)
13. Oliveira, J.P.S.E., et al.: In silico investigation of the effects of distinct temporal patterns of electrical stimulation to the amygdala using a network of izhikevich neurons. In: Latin American Workshop on Computational Neuroscience, pp. 132–152. Springer (2021)

14. Pena, R.F., Zaks, M.A., Roque, A.C.: Dynamics of spontaneous activity in random networks with multiple neuron subtypes and synaptic noise: spontaneous activity in networks with synaptic noise. J. Comput. Neurosci. **45**, 1–28 (2018)
15. Robbins, H.: Some aspects of the sequential design of experiments. Bull. Am. Math. Soc. **58**(5), 527–535 (1952)
16. Savage, N.: Epidemiology: the complexities of epilepsy. Nature **511**(7508) (2014)
17. Spencer, S.S.: When should temporal-lobe epilepsy be treated surgically? Lancet Neurol. **1**(6), 375–382 (2002)
18. Sutton, R.S., Barto, A.G.: Reinforcement Learning: An Introduction. MIT press (2018)

Fuzzy Control with Central Pattern Generators for the Locomotion of Quadruped Robotic Systems

Edgar-Mario Rico-Mesa[1]([✉]) [iD] and Jesús-Antonio Hernández-Riveros[2] [iD]

[1] Dpto. Electricidad Industrial, Centro Tecnología de la Manufactura Avanzada, SENA, Street 104, 69-120, Medellin 050042, Antioquia, Colombia
emrico@sena.edu.co

[2] Dpto. Energía Eléctrica y Automática, Facultad de Minas, Universidad Nacional de Colombia, Career 80, 65-223, Medellin 050036, Antioquia, Colombia
jahernan@unal.edu.co

Abstract. The development with CPG of the locomotion of a quadruped robot with three degrees of freedom per leg and its management by fuzzy control is presented. The robot, simulated in Gazebo-ROS, has three proximity sensors, an IMU sensor, and an odometry sensor. The purpose of the robot is the execution of locomotion in different types of movement. To reproduce the motor function of locomotion the central pattern generators use a novel mathematical model. The robot's environment is a labyrinth on a flat surface. A three-level control architecture operates the robot's locomotion. At levels I and II, the motor function of locomotion is reproduced with central pattern generators. Level III plans locomotion movement. This level has parallel control of both obstacle avoidance with a fuzzy controller and robot stability with a central pattern generator. The priority in motion planning is the stability of the robot. The proper functioning of the robot control architecture is demonstrated.

Keywords: Central Pattern Generators · Stability · Reflex Movements · Fuzzy Control · Quadruped Robot · Gazebo ROS

1 Introduction

The control of mobile robots with wheels was one of the leading areas of robotics in the last century. Therefore, it is the type of robot that has evolved the most technologically and that has had a great preponderance in researching work, given that on environments with flat surfaces or low topographic accidents, their movements are effective, fast, and precise to the point that there are currently collaborative applications with humans [1]. However, the control of articulated

R.-M. Edgar-Mario and H.-R. Jesús-Antonio—These authors contributed equally to this work.

robotic systems has become a topic of great importance in recent years given the great possibilities of its implementation in terrestrial exploration under extreme conditions due to specific circumstances such as cataclysms, accidents, or environments not suitable for humans, or surfaces with broken topography, where mobile robotics with wheels cannot move easily [2]. It should be noted that the degree of complexity of the locomotion control of an articulated quadruped robot is greater to the extent that the number of degrees of freedom per leg is considerable; thus, typically, the quadruped robots that have been developed in the 21st century for locomotion are made up of two degrees of freedom (two joints) per leg. Although in the last five years work has begun with quadruped robots with three degrees of freedom per leg, increasing the degree of complexity in locomotion control but gaining greater versatility in the performance of these robots in unstructured environments [3]. In this project, a quadruped robot was developed on a high-capacity simulation platform called ROS-Gazebo, with an environment in which physical laws are considered. The robot is built from the basic geometric elements of Gazebo. The structure of the robot consists of three joints linked by three rectangular prisms that make up each leg and a shell that corresponds to a cubic prism with square faces. The robot has internal sensors such as the inertial moment unit introduced into its body to determine stability issues, torque and force sensors located in its joints to determine efforts produced in collisions with obstacles. The robot has external sensors such as ultrasound and infrared proximity sensors to determine the distance of obstacles, odometry sensors to determine the position of the robot in a certain environment [4].

Gazebo simulation technology operates with ROS (Robot System Operating). Gazebo is defined as a three-dimensional dynamic simulator that has the ability to represent different types of robots with great accuracy and effectiveness in environments of considerable complexity. ROS has been described as a meta-operating system that runs on top of the Linux operating system. It is important to indicate that ROS becomes a workspace for the development of robot software that provides the designer with a series of tools, libraries, conventions, which make it easy to create robotic applications with a high degree of robustness [5]. To shape the locomotion of the quadruped robot, the coordination of movement of each leg and the synchronization of movement of the four legs were established as motor functions that are produced by central pattern generators (CPG) located as oscillators in the joints and in the central system. The CPG are made up of its own recurrent neural networks that are built from a unique mathematical model. Sten Grillner proposed central pattern generators to explain the behavior of motor functions in living beings [6]. For short-term motion planning of the robot's locomotion based on an objective, such as the typical case of avoiding obstacles in a maze, a control module based on fuzzy logic has been created, such as an intelligent brain module that It allows effective and intuitive development of the robot's locomotion. This type of control was developed by Lotfi Zadeh [7] seeking to imitate human behavior in its control actions based on qualitative values described in fuzzy input and output sets, robot operation rules, and an inference machine, whose result of its application are smooth movements with a very natural and high percentage of assertiveness.

1.1 Brief Review of Works in Quadruped Locomotion Control

In the review of works that have been published in international journals in the last three years on the topic of this paper, the following has been found: in the document titled "Adaptive gait planning for quadruped robot based on the center of inertia over rough terrain" a series of experiments are carried out to investigate the gait of a quadruped robot on three different surfaces: flat, rough, and steep slope. To determine the robot's stability, the zero-moment point criterion is used, which guarantees the stable gait of the quadruped robot [8]. The paper "Hybrid learning mechanisms under a neural control network for various walking speed generation of a quadruped robot" presents a neural control framework to integrate probability-based black box optimization (PIBB) and supervised learning for the generation of motor patterns of robots with different walking speeds. The structure of the control framework is based on a combination of a central pattern generator (CPG), a premotor network based on a radial basis function (RBF) and a hypernetwork, configuring a CPG-RBF hypercontrol neural network [9]. In the paper "Modeling Quadruped Leg Dynamics on Deformable Terrains using Data-driven Koopman Operators," an experimental framework is proposed to obtain a data-based Koopman model of the dynamics of the legs of a quadruped on deformable terrains as a switched dynamic system. By implementing the switched system model in the robot (taking advantage of the linearity of the Koopman operator), it was possible to predict walking trajectories in an unknown terrain [10]. In the paper "Neuromorphic adaptive spiking CPG towards bio-inspired locomotion" a bioinspired locomotion mechanism is proposed that includes adaptability to any change that arises in the environment. Therefore, central pattern generators are used for the execution of motor functions and the Feedback is obtained through FSR (Force Sensitive Resistive) sensors [11]. The study "Prismatic Quasi-Direct-Drives for dynamic quadruped locomotion with high payload capacity" present a quadruped robot with prismatic leg driven by quasi-direct drives (QDDs) with large payload capacity in dynamic locomotion. Instead of typical leg mechanisms using articulated joints, QDDs are integrated with the belt-driven linear mechanism to achieve prismatic leg movement [12]. The paper "Synthesizing the optimal gait of a quadruped robot with soft actuators using deep reinforcement learning" proposes a new design of quadruped robots that use soft actuators driven by tendons on all four legs. To achieve locomotion, the flexible components of the quadruped robot are initially used and modeled with different finite element methods and lumped parameters, and the model accuracy and calculation efficiency are also analyzed. Gentle actor-critic and curricular learning methods are then applied to learn optimal walking modes for different walking tasks. Finally, the learned steps are implemented in a robot to carry hand tools [13].

2   Methods

The quadruped robot used in this work is developed on an open platform that simulates real conditions of the movements. To generate the displacement, the CPG and the specifically designed fuzzy controller are added by programming. The simulation platform is composed of the GAZEBO-ROS packages.

2.1   ROS

ROS stands for Robot Operating System; it is a software platform or workspace for developing specialized software for robotics projects. It was developed by the Willow Garage Research Institute in 2007 under the BSD license; all programs on this platform are open source (OSS), and its use is free across the board. The ROS system was created taking into account other existing open software platforms such as OpenCV, Player/Stage, Gazebo, Orocos/KDL, among others. ROS is made up of a set of programming libraries, applications, drivers, and visualization, monitoring, simulation, and analysis tools, all reusable for the development of new applications for both simulated and real robots. Additionally, ROS also provides standard services typical of an operating system that is mainly installed on Ubuntu. It has its own package manager using commands from the terminal for the management, compilation, and execution of files, as well as hardware abstraction [14].

2.2   GAZEBO

Gazebo is a 3D simulator in which kinematic and dynamic behaviors operate. It supports the presence of multiple robots in complex, indoor or outdoor, realistic, and three-dimensional environments. Among its features we can name the following: Gazebo is free software supported by Willow Garage, and can be reconfigured, expanded, and modified, Gazebo can be run from ROS with APIs to control the robots in simulations, that is, send and receive data from the Gazebo built environment. In simulations, robots can interact with the world since the laws of classical physics are incorporated. There is the possibility of creating simulation scenarios (worlds), varying the characteristics of contacts with the ground, obstacles and even values of gravity in three dimensions. It also contains multiple plugins to add sensors to the robot model and simulate them, such as odometry, GPS, IMU, force, contact, proximity sensors, lasers, and stereo cameras [15].

2.3   CPG Models

In the development of movement coordination in articulated mobile robotics, several algorithms have been implemented based on the concepts and theories of biologists and researchers such as Avis Cohen, Serge Rossignol and Sten Grillner. Advanced models that imitate CPGs use, among others, recurrent artificial neural networks (RANN). These neural networks are not based on knowledge of the positions of the joints in space but act directly on the joints. A prior study of the kinematics of the robot's movement is not necessary. The Continuous Time Recurrent Neural Networks (CTRAAN) architecture consists of neural networks that have bidirectional connections between nodes (Fig. 1) in such a way that they allow the reproduction of oscillatory and transient signals in the absence of an external signal, known as the model Hertz, Krogh and Palmer [16].

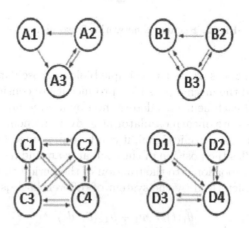

Fig. 1. Neural network structures for CPG.

The mathematical representation of recurrent neural networks is a system of first-order differential equations, such as the one presented in Eq. 1 with i = 1...M.

$$\tau_i * dy_i/dt = -y_i + \sum_{j=1}^{m} w_{ij} * \sigma(y_i + \theta_j) + I_i \qquad (1)$$

The state function of each neuron based on the Chiel-Beer Model is generally made up of five parameters: time constant (τ) associated with the permittivity of the cell membrane, weights of synaptic connections between neurons (w), point of operation of each node (θ), transfer function of each neuron (σ) and external input to the system (I). The typical models most used by biologists for CPG representation are the 2- and 4-neuron models [17].

2.3.1 Two-Neuron CPG Model

This model presents mathematical schemes that imitate the behavior of a system of two coupled oscillators that seek to show the way in which biological oscillators influence each other. Each oscillator can represent a neuron or a network of cells that function collectively as an oscillator. The specific mathematical model proposed by Rand, Cohen and Holmes is considered for a network of two oscillators

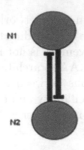

Fig. 2. Recurrent network of two neurons

(Fig. 2), where each one is treated as a simple biological oscillator, if the structure of the oscillator and the mechanisms that produce it are considered [18].

The behavior of each neuron is determined by a large number of parameters that represents the state of each oscillator at a given moment. However, since its response corresponds to a cyclic signal, it can be represented by a single variable, i ϵ 2,3, which specifies the position of the oscillator around its limit cycle at time t. Therefore, it is proportional to the fraction of the period that has elapsed, and its behavior is characterized by the system of differential Eqs. 2 and 3.

$$\dot{\theta}_1(t) = w_1 + h_{12}(\theta_1, \theta_2) \tag{2}$$

$$\dot{\theta}_2(t) = w_2 + h_{21}(\theta_2, \theta_1) \tag{3}$$

Where $h_{ij}(\theta_i, \theta_j)$ represents the periodic coupling effect between the j_{th} oscillator and the i_{th} oscillator.

2.3.2   Four-Neuron CPG Model

This release examines a model consisting of chains of four oscillators with nearest neighbor coupling, as well as more complex architectures with different types of coupling between the four oscillatory cells (Fig. 3).

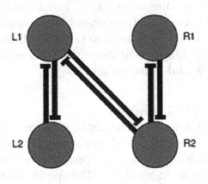

Fig. 3. Recurrent network of four neurons.

The following approach in Eqs. 4, 5, 6 and 7 is proposed by Rand [18] more generally for n oscillator chains, which is adapted for a system of four differential equations.

$$\dot{\theta}_1(t) = w_1 + h_{12}(\theta_1, \theta_2) \tag{4}$$

$$\dot{\theta}_2(t) = w_2 + h_{12}(\theta_1, \theta_2) + h_{23}(\theta_2, \theta_3) \tag{5}$$

$$\dot{\theta}_3(t) = w_3 + h_{32}(\theta_3, \theta_2) + h_{34}(\theta_3, \theta_4) \tag{6}$$

$$\dot{\theta}_4(t) = w_4 + h_{43}(\theta_4, \theta_3) \tag{7}$$

The oscillators at the two ends of the chain are subject to the influence of a single neighboring cell, so they behave slightly differently than the internal cells of the chain, where they are influenced by two neighbors. The model generates the path of the contracted wave at a constant speed without the presence of a frequency gradient in the oscillator pattern according to Kopell and Ermentrout [18].

2.3.3 New CPG Model

The mathematical model that we have developed was based on the CPG model presented previously. For its consolidation, recurrent neural networks have initially been developed from systems of specific first-order differential equations [19,20], and [21]. From these specific cases, a general mathematical model was built, which is presented below in Eqs. 8, 9 and 10.

$\forall \; i \; \epsilon \; Z \wedge (A, B, C, D, k_1, k_2, \tau_i) \; \epsilon \; R$

$| \; i=1$

$$\tau_i * dy_i/dt = -y_i + \frac{A(k_1 - D * y_{i+1})^2}{((k_1 + D * y_{i+1})^2 + (k_1 - D * y_i)^2)} \tag{8}$$

$| \; 1 < i < n$

$$\tau_i * dy_i/dt = -y_i + \frac{A(k_2 - D * y_{i-1})^2}{((k_2 - D * y_{i+1})^2 + (k_2 + D * y_i)^2)} \tag{9}$$

$| \; i=n$

$$\tau_i * dy_i/dt = -y_i + \frac{A(B - C * y_{n-1})^2}{((B - C * y_n)^2 + (B + C * y_{n-1})^2)} \tag{10}$$

The first application of this model has been carried out on a dog-type robot in [22].

2.4 Fuzzy Systems

This is a flexible computing technique that allows a processing system to classify real-world information on an infinite scale bounded by true and false values. Its objective is to provide formal mathematical support for approximate reasoning that makes use of propositions that express imprecise information [23].

2.4.1 Fuzzy Control

This control modeling is used to manipulate the fundamental variable of the plant that is expressed in terms of linguistic variables. It acts in accordance with decisions that are inferred from linguistic rules proposed by an expert. The structure of a fuzzy control is shown in Fig. 4 and each of its components (fuzzification, rule set, inference machine, and defuzzification) will be explained below.

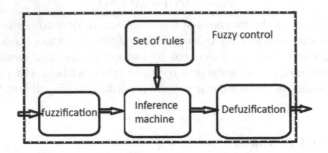

Fig. 4. Structure of a fuzzy controller

Fuzzification: It consists of classifying a physical variable according to the knowledge we have about its behavior. This classification is qualitative and is represented by areas, usually in a triangular and trapezoidal shape. The names assigned to these areas represent the linguistic variables; the height that these areas have is called the membership function (μ) and varies from 0 to 1, or from 0 to 255, etc. This depends on the system designer, and the width corresponds to the numerical values of the physical variable.

Rules: The rules are a set of parameters (related to a physical variable that will allow control over the system). They reflect the knowledge that the designer has about the process that he/she wants to control and indicate the most optimal decisions with which he/she wants to control the main variable of the plant. Each rule is made up of two parts:

- The antecedent corresponds to the linguistic variable where the activated input physical variables are found.
- The consequent corresponds to the linguistic variable of the physical output variable where the decision made is found.

This implication depends on the knowledge that the designer has about the operation of the plant (see Table 1).

Inference Machine: It is the process by which calculations are carried out to find a specific value (weight), which is achieved by applying the concepts corresponding to operations with fuzzy sets (such as max, min, product, sum), whose interpretation depends on the designer's intention. At this stage, the most appropriate weights are obtained that will indicate the decision to be made.

Defuzzification: It consists of classifying the physical variable according to the

Table 1. Some examples of rules

Antecedent	Consequent
If the set point is low and the error is negative $\mu B \cap N$	The motor must have small speed decreases μD
In mathematical form it is: $\mu B \cap N \rightarrow \mu D$	
If the error is 0 regardless of the set point $\mu Z \cap X$	The motor must maintain the current speed μM
In mathematical form it is: $\mu Z \cap X \rightarrow \mu M$	
If the set point is high and the error is positive $\mu A \cap P$	The motor must have large speed increases μAu
In mathematical form it is: $\mu A \cap P \rightarrow \mu Au$	

way you want to control the plant, that is, according to the designer's criteria. The classification is done qualitatively, each linguistic variable is assigned an area, usually in a triangular or trapezoidal shape, the height of the areas or the membership function varies from 0 to 1 or from 0 to 255. Through this stage, the aim is to translate the weights (values that correspond to the membership function) into terms of the physical variable that is being manipulated [24].

3 Results

3.1 Robot Quadruped

The structure of the quadruped robot was built in ROS-GAZEBO (Fig. 5A) whose parts are based on the primitive geometry such as the body and link. The body is a straight cylinder. Link 1 consists of a straight cylinder, links 2 and 3 with a prism with four rectangular faces (see Fig. 5B). Sensors, such as the odometer and proximity sensors, are fixed on the robot body.

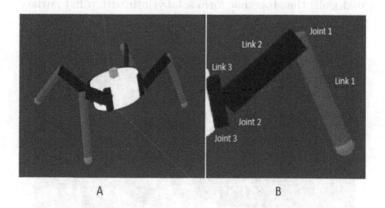

Fig. 5. Robot quadruped A) Complete quadruped robot designed in ROS - GAZEBO. B) Robot leg joints

Although it is possible to import mechanical designs from packages such as Solid Edge, Solid Work or AutoCAD into ROS - GAZEBO, it is also possible to implement hardware with primitive elements without requiring knowledge of mechanical design. In addition, the configuration of the sensing devices is simple and easy without the need for advanced electronics knowledge. These two aspects allow both the electronic engineer and the mechanical engineer to access this type of simulators in which the basic knowledge to be able to use it is programming. Some sensors have been located on the body of the robot, such as the IMU, which is located in the center of the body on the square-faced cube (see Fig. 6A), while the ultrasound proximity sensor is located at the rear (see Fig. 6B) and the infrared proximity sensors are located on the front, both on the right (Fig. 6C) and on the left (Fig. 6D).

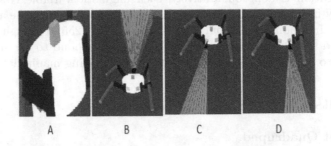

Fig. 6. Sensors of the quadruped robot A) IMU sensor (Phosphorescent pink cube). B)Central posterior ultrasound sensor. C) Right front infrared sensor (phosphorescent blue cube). D)Front left infrared sensor (phosphorescent green cube).

3.2   Robot Environment

The environment with which the robot interacts is made up of a series of randomly located walls that together form a labyrinth with a flat surface with low friction (see Fig. 7).

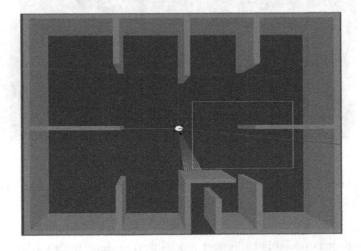

Fig. 7. Labyrinth-like built environment

It is important to indicate that the intention of the developed environment is to identify the robot's response capacity in complex spaces, a typical situation in scenarios with difficult access and low mobility. In this type of environments, articulated robots have great potential to operate and meet the objectives set if they have an optimal control module.

3.3   Control Architecture

The control module developed for the quadruped robot is composed of a three-level architecture where each level has a specific function, Fig. 8.

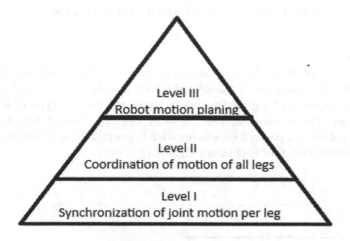

Fig. 8. Locomotion control architecture

3.3.1   Level I

The specific turns of each joint based on the movement of the leg corresponds to Level I. The intention is to achieve synchronization of the joints that make up the leg. Each type of locomotion performs a combination of joint movements with different execution times. The mechanism used to meet the objective at this level is the application of central generators of patterns represented with Recurrent Neural Networks (RNR) of three neurons that reproduce three oscillatory signals (Fig. 9).

The light blue signal (neuron 1) is responsible for activating joint 1 when the amplitude is maximum relative to point A (Fig. 9). The yellow signal (neuron 2) is responsible for activating joint 2 when the amplitude is maximum relative to point B (Fig. 9). The green signal (neuron 3) is responsible for activating joint 3 when the amplitude is maximum relative to point C (Fig. 9). The mathematical module used is a system of three first-order differential equations with $n = 3$ that was obtained from the general model Eqs. 8, 9, and 10. Its parameters are in Table 2.

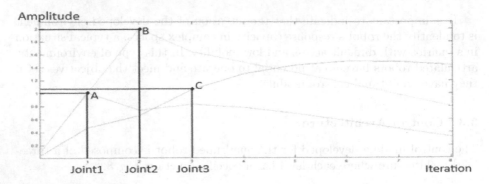

Fig. 9. Oscillatory RNR signals from three neurons

3.3.2   Level II

Level II corresponds to the movements of each leg depending on the type of locomotion. The execution of transitions occurs at this level. The intention is to achieve coordination of leg movements to cause the desired type of locomotion or transition. The mechanism used to meet the objective at this level is the application of central pattern generators with Recurrent Neural Networks (RNR) of four neurons with four oscillatory signals (Fig. 10).

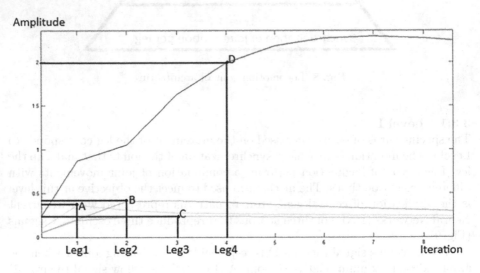

Fig. 10. Oscillatory RNR signals from four neurons

The yellow signal (neuron 1) is responsible for activating leg 1 when the amplitude is maximum relative at point A (Fig. 10). The green signal (neuron 2) activates leg 2 when the amplitude is maximum relative to point B (Fig. 10). The light blue signal (neuron 3) activates leg 3 when the amplitude is maximum relative at point C (Fig. 10). The dark blue signal (neuron 4) activates leg 4 when the amplitude is maximum relative at point D (Fig. 10). The mathematical structure used is a system of four first-order differential equations with n = 4 obtained from the general model Eqs. 8, 9, and 10. The parameter values are presented in Table 2.

3.3.3   Level III

Level III corresponds to the robot's locomotion movements to avoid obstacles and avoid overturning situations. The intention is to achieve robot motion control with fuzzy logic. Fuzzy control performs short-term displacement planning to avoid obstacles and articulates reflex movements to avoid possible instabilities of the robot. The mechanism used to achieve this objective is the development of reflex movements through central pattern generators with Recurrent Neural Networks (RNR) of two neurons, which produce two oscillatory signals (Fig. 11).

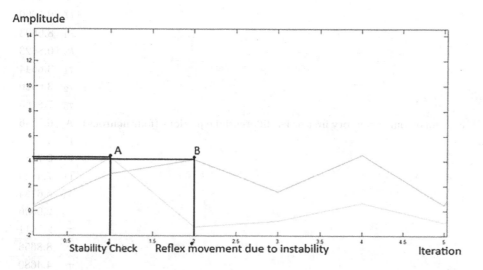

Fig. 11. Oscillatory RNR signals from two neurons

The light yellow signal (neuron 1) activates the stability check when the amplitude is maximum relative to point A (Fig. 11). The light blue signal (neuron 2) activates the reflex movement due to instability when the amplitude is maximum relative to point B (Fig. 11). The mathematical structure used to reproduce the CPG is a system of two first-order differential equations with n − 2 obtained from the general model Eqs. 8, 9, and 10, with the parameter values presented in Table 2.

The recurrent neural network of two neurons is being always executed, including the moment in which the control action is incorporated into the robot's locomotion. This mechanism has priority over the execution of fuzzy control

Table 2. Parameters of systems of first-order differential equations

Equation Name	Parameters	
System of two oscillatory first-order differential equations (two neurons)	A	5.4389
	B	7.2105
	C	5.2250
	D	9.9370
	k_1	2.1868
	k_2	1.0580
	τ_1	1.0970
	τ_2	0.6359
System of three oscillatory first-order differential equations (three neurons)	A	7.4003
	B	2.3483
	C	7.3496
	D	9.7060
	k_1	8.6693
	k_2	0.8623
	τ_1	3.6644
	τ_2	3.6920
	τ_3	7.8465
System of four oscillatory first order differential equations (four neurons)	A	6.5346
	B	4.8966
	C	9.7285
	D	7.4849
	k_1	5.6784
	k_2	2.9896
	τ_1	2.5611
	τ_2	8.8656
	τ_3	4.4680
	τ_4	8.1599

for obstacle avoidance, since it is essential that adequate stability of the robot is maintained at all times. For the execution of reflex movement control, three types of situations were established. The first situation has to do with the robot having total stability, in which case the priority is obstacle avoidance. The second case is that the robot presents marginal stability; under this circumstance the action to be developed is a transition to less rapid locomotion. The third moment is the detection of instability of the robot, whose immediate action is to stop the robot for a few seconds until stability is recovered. It should be noted that the control of reflex movements and the fuzzy control for obstacle avoidance are worked in parallel (Fig. 12).

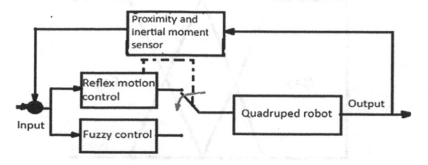

Fig. 12. Level III: Control diagram

In the fuzzy control, an analysis was made of the robot's locomotion to determine the input variables, the output variables, and the set of rules with their processing in the inference machine. The input variables were defined according to the function that the robot performs, in our case it is obstacle avoidance: Therefore, two infrared proximity sensors are proposed at the ends of the front part of the robot given that for colors other than black, regardless of whether they are flat or profiled, their response is optimal, and, an ultrasonic sensor in the middle of the back of the robot taking into account that its function will be decisive at close distances between the robot and obstacles. Regarding the output variable, the function to be fulfilled of avoiding obstacles has been taken into account. More than the form of movement, in this function, the rotation movement of the robot on itself is essential, to change its course and thus avoid the obstacle. Regarding the set of rules and the application of the inference machine, 27 rules have been established with their respective antecedents and consequences and their operation through the inference machine through the Max and Min operators. The fuzzification of the input data from the three proximity sensors (Central posterior ultrasound sensor, Right front infrared sensor, Front left infrared sensor) have the same three fuzzy sets whose linguistic variables are: Near, Intermediate and Far. It is important to note that the maximum obstacle identification distance is two meters, and the minimum distance is 0.1 m. The Near label is assigned to sensor values that are in the interval [0, 1.0], its fuzzy set has a trapezoidal shape. The Intermediate label is assigned to an interval between 0.5 mt and 1.5 mt, its fuzzy set has a triangular shape. The Far label is defined for distances greater than or equal to 1 m, its fuzzy set has a trapezoidal shape (see Fig. 13).

It is important to indicate that the weight assigned to the physical variable that activates a certain linguistic variable is obtained from the linear equation $y = Ax + B$, which is applied to the contours of the fuzzy sets. ultrasound sensor. Regarding the defuzzification over the output variable Rotation, it was

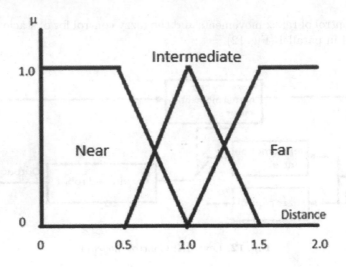

Fig. 13. Input fuzzification.

constructed with five fuzzy sets that correspond to the linguistic variables: do not rotate, rotate 45°C to the left, rotate 90°C to the left, rotate 45°C to the right, rotate 90°C to the right. The label "do not rotate" has the interval [−35, 35] of the output variable. The rotate 45°C counterclockwise label is between −80°C and −10°C. The label "rotate 90°C left" is in the range [−125, −55]. The rotate 45°C clockwise label ranges from 10°C to 80°C. The rotate 90°C clockwise label is between 55°C and 125°C. It should also be indicated that the sign of the output data means the orientation of the rotation, in this case if the control result is positive, in the algorithm it means turning to the right, and if it is negative, it means turning to the left. All output fuzzy sets have a triangular shape (See Fig. 14).

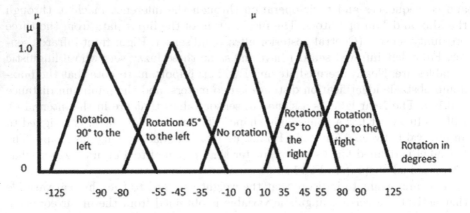

Fig. 14. Output defuzzyfication

To define the output value of the fuzzy control, a weighting value is used with the activated output sets obtained by the inference machine that determines an area that may contain several fuzzy sets. Therefore, to know with certainty the output value of the control in terms of the output variable "rotation", the centroid method is used. In programming, this method is applied discretely and approximately to Eq. 11.

$$fxy = \frac{\int yfy\,dy}{\int fy\,dy} \tag{11}$$

In the construction of the set of rules, the knowledge of the expert or designer about the behavior and capabilities of the robot was important, also considering the different combinations of situations that arise with proximity sensors, as shown in Table 3.

Table 3. Set of rules

Premise	Input									Output				
Rule	rear ultrasonic sensor			front left infrared sensor			front right infrared sensor			Rotation Rotation				
N°	Near	Interme-diate	Far	Near	Inter-diate	Far	Near	Interme-diate	Far	Rotate 90° left	Rotate 45° left	No rotation	Rotate 45° right	Rotate 90° right
1			x			x			x			x		
2			x			x		x			x			
3			x			x	x						x	
4			x		x				x	x				
5			x		x			x			x			
6			x		x		x							x
7			x	x					x					x
8			x	x				x						x
9			x	x			x			x				
10		x				x			x			x		
11		x				x		x			x			
12		x				x	x					x		
13		x			x				x					x
14		x			x			x		x				
15		x			x		x			x				
16		x		x					x					x
17		x		x				x		x				
18		x		x			x						x	
19	x					x			x			x		
20	x					x		x					x	
21	x					x	x						x	
22	x				x				x	x				
23	x				x			x				x		
24	x				x		x						x	
25	x			x					x	x				
26	x			x				x		x				
27	x			x			x							x

The interpretation of Table 3 is the following: the antecedent is formed with the inputs and the consequent with the outputs, let us take rule 1: if rear obstacle is far and left front obstacle is far and right front obstacle is far then the robot does not must rotate. The other 26 rules defined in Table 3 are interpreted in the same way. The inference machine operates the rules that are activated according to the input data applied by the Max and Min operators, taking into account that the rules have the same output action in common, in this way a certain weight is obtained as a result. The weight value assigned to the respective output ranges between 0 and 1. Below is an example from the rules presented in Table 3. Suppose that rules 6 and 7 are activated, since they have the same output action then the following mathematical procedure is applied:

Let s1', s2', s3' be inputs of the rear sensor, front right sensor and front left sensor, respectively.

So

(s1'xs2'xs3')o(LxCxL→R90D)∪(s1'xs2'xs3')o(LxCxI→R90D)

Is equivalent to:

(s1'xs2'xs3')o(LxCxL→R90D) = Sups1(μs1'*μL)*sups2(μs2'*μC)*sups3(μs3'*μL)*μR90D

And

(s1'xs2'xs3')o(LxCxI→R90D)= Sups1(μs1'μL)*sups2(μs2'*μC)*sups3(μs3'*μI)*μR90D

Replacing them with their respective operators, we have: Max(Min(μs1'*μL, μs2'*μC,μs3'*μL)*μR90D,Min(μs1'*μL,μs2'*μC,μs3'*μI)*μR90D).

Finally, the weights corresponding to each linguistic variable are assigned and the operators are executed. First, the minimum between the three weights is found separately and then the maximum is found between the two results obtained by applying the minimum.

Let

s1'*μL= 0.4,μs2'*μC=0.7,μs3'*μL=0.3,μs3'*μI=0.1

Then we replace in the expression like this

Max(Min(0.4, 0.7,0.3)* μ R90D, Min(0.4, 0.7, 0.1)* μ R90D).

Therefore

Max((0.3)* μR90D,(0.1)* μR90D)

The result is:

(0.3)*μR90D

The result is interpreted like this: the activated fuzzy set is rotate 90° to the right with weight of 0.3.

Figure 15 shows a test operation of the quadruped robot in the labyrinth created in the GAZEBO simulator, with the movement footprint of the robot. Each value in both axes, x and y, is in meters. The robot performed a displacement of 30 forward locomotion cycles (Fig. 15A) and 60 forward locomotion cycles (Fig. 15B) between the init point (Start) and the endpoint (Finish). The control architecture implemented in the robot prioritizes its stability over obstacle avoidance. By briefly monitoring the path traveled by the robot, its intention is to avoid possible obvious collisions with the walls that make up the labyrinth.

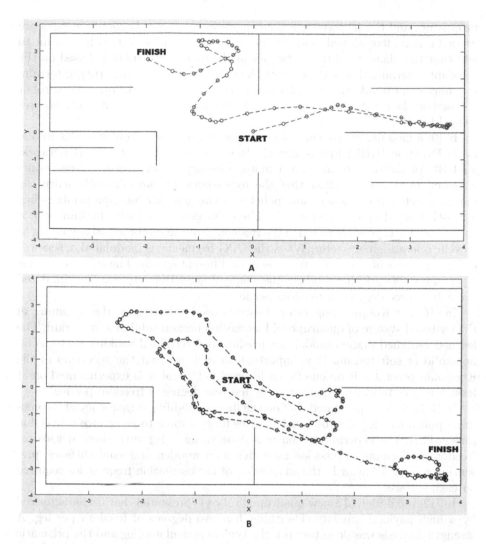

Fig. 15. Robot operation in labyrinth. A)30 cycles of locomotion. B) 60 cycles of locomotion.

4 Discussion

To make a comparative analysis between the work of this project with recent publications of similar robotic systems, some details of the works found in databases of great importance worldwide are presented below.

In [8] an adaptive omnidirectional walk is designed for a quadruped robot with three degrees of freedom per leg on rugged terrain. Walking is a type of static gait in which the best stability is sought through the virtual support plane that allows determining the zero-moment point. This procedure simplifies data processing, and the performance is adequate in real time. Locomotion tests are carried out on flat, sloped, and sloping and rugged surfaces. It is important to add that the planning of the static gait of the quadruped robot is based on the constant determination of the center of inertia as it advances over rugged terrain. It is important to add that the planning of the static gait of the quadruped robot is based on the constant determination of the center of inertia as it advances over rugged terrain.

In [9] a modular neural control system is proposed based on the CPG-Radial Basis Function (RBF) hyper-network. It is a combination of a CPG network, an RBF premotor network and a motor memory hyper-network. The results obtained in simulation show that the hyper-network can efficiently learn the mapping between frequencies and policies. It can generate an appropriate policy for both trained and unused speeds. The CPG generates basic rhythmic motor signals, and it is possible to refine the frequency of the motor signal according to a cyclic operating parameter. When the CPG frequency is modulated, a series of oscillators are achieved that can be used for different speeds. The RBF network is a premotor network that modifies the shape of the CPG outputs. The simulated robot has three degrees of freedom per leg.

In [10] the Koopman operator theory is used to recognize the dynamics of the switched system of quadrupedal locomotion on non-solid or soft terrain. The learned switched system model can predict undetermined walking patterns on non-solid or soft terrain. It is important to indicate that the spectrum of the Koopman generator is unique for each terrain. The robot is experimented on at least four soft terrains. The robot only has one degree of freedom per leg.

In [11] a CPG is presented that on the fly can modify the frequency of locomotion applied to a leg of a robot using as feedback a force-to-resistance conversion sensor FSR, the experimentation was done using a leg with three degrees of freedom performing locomotion movements on wooden and sand surfaces, presenting robust behavior in the adaptation of the oscillation frequencies required on each surface.

In [12] the design of a new quadruped robot is presented that is characterized by a high payload capacity. The robot has two degrees of freedom per leg. A strength analysis was done between the typical articulated leg and the prismatic leg, finding a better response capacity in the prismatic leg. Therefore, the robot is equipped with prismatic legs. Dynamic control is used for locomotion that allows it to jog at an average speed of $0.7 \, \text{m/s}$ and a payload identification method with the capacity to lift a payload of $125 \, \text{kg}$. The robot performed locomotion on flat surfaces.

In [13] a quadruped robot design enabled by four smooth continuous actuators driven by tendons is proposed. The robot has two degrees of freedom per leg. The robot is simulated and staged on flat surfaces. Reinforcement learning and Soft Actor-Critic techniques are used to reproduce walking locomotion. In addition, we sought to vary the speed of locomotion using the curricular learning method, although certain differences were found in the speed of locomotion between the simulation and the real robotic system.

The quadruped robot of this project is based on simulations in the GAZEBO ROS software. The robot has 3 degrees of freedom per leg. Locomotion control is made up of a three-level architecture. The first two levels focus on the synchronization of joint rotation and the coordination of leg movement; For this purpose, the central pattern generators use a novel mathematical model to reproduce the motor function of locomotion. The third level is oriented to the planning of locomotion in which reflex movement control is used, executed by a central pattern generator and a fuzzy controller for obstacle avoidance. In the control of reflex movements, the transition between types of locomotion is used to maintain stability. The robot is simulated in a flat labyrinth-like environment.

In general terms, in the cited works the concern is observed to perfect the motor function of locomotion, focusing mostly on the development of a certain locomotion, basically walking, or trotting, using different techniques or methods of computational intelligence. In some of the works mentioned, variations in the hardware of the limbs are proposed with the intention of seeking alternatives with better performance in locomotion. However, if you want to have a greater capacity for response and a greater scope in the face of unknown environments, it is important to have different locomotion alternatives, a safe transition between them, have the ability to respond immediately to possible rollover hazards, and have locomotion planning, with a low computational cost. It is in this sense that this project has focused, clearly proposing a control infrastructure that promotes safe and robust locomotion, making the most of computational intelligence to approximate the locomotion of terrestrial quadrupedal living beings.

5   Conclusion

In the GAZEBO-ROS simulator, a quadruped robot with three degrees of freedom per leg and three proximity sensors has been developed from primitive geometric elements. However, programming knowledge is required to build the robot.

The configuration of the control module of a quadruped robot with twelve degrees of freedom in its four legs is highly complex, so in this work, a three-level control architecture was proposed. With central pattern generators in the first two levels, the locomotion motor function is configured for the synchronization of turns of the joints of each leg and the coordination of the movements of the four legs according to the movement to be executed. On the other hand, the third level fulfills the double function of planning movements focused on avoiding obstacles through fuzzy control and applying reflex movements to prevent the robot from overturning.

The simulation carried out with the quadruped robots in an unknown environment, such as a labyrinth, fulfilled the objective set in the movement planning since there were no real problems of overturning or collisions of the robot in the proposed environment. This demonstrates the controller's ability to manage potential risks that arise during robot locomotion.

References

1. Shneier, M., Bostelman, R.: Literature review of mobile robots for manufacturing. In: National Institute of Standards and Technology. U.S. Department of Commerce (2015). https://doi.org/10.6028/NIST.IR.8022
2. Ajwad, S.A., Ullah, M.I., Baizid, K., Iqbal, J.: A comprehensive state-of-the-art on control of industrial articulated robots. J. Balk. Tribological Assoc. **20**(4), 499–521 (2014)
3. Lan, K.: A study on control algorithm for robots with multi-degree of freedom. J. Phys. Conf. Ser. **13459**(4), 042089 (2019). https://doi.org/10.1088/1742-6596/1345/4/042089
4. Merlan, M.: Robot Operating System (ROS). The Complete Reference. Springer, Switzerland (2023)
5. Takaya, K., Asai, T., Kroumov, V., Smarandache, F.: Simulation environment for mobile robots testing using ROS and Gazebo. Paper presented at the 20th international conference on system theory, control and computing (ICSTCC), Sinaia, Romania, 13–15 October 2016 (2016)
6. Grillner, S., Wallan, P.: Central pattern generators for locomotion, with special reference to vertebrates. Annu. Rev. Neurosci. **8**, 233–261 (1985). https://doi.org/10.1146/annurev.ne.08.030185.001313
7. Zadeh, L.A.: Fuzzy sets. Inf. Control **8**(3), 338–353 (1965). https://doi.org/10.1016/S0019-9958(65)90241-X
8. Chen, J., Xu, K., Ding, X.: Adaptive gait planning for quadruped robot based on center of inertia over rough terrain. Biomimetic Intel. Robot. **2**(1), 100031 (2022). https://doi.org/10.1016/j.birob.2021.100031
9. Zhang, Y., Thor, M., Dilokthanakul, N., Dai, Z.: Hybrid learning mechanisms under a neural control network for various walking speed generation of a quadruped robot. Neural Netw. **167**, 292–308 (2023). https://doi.org/10.1016/j.neunet.2023.08.030
10. Krolicki, A., Rufino, D., Zheng, A., Narayanan, S.S.K.S., Erb, J., Vaidya, U.: Modeling quadruped leg dynamics on deformable terrains using data-driven Koopman operators. Paper presented at the 2nd modeling, estimation and control conference, MECC 2022, Jersey City, NJ, USA, 2–5 October 2022 (2022)
11. López-Osorio, P., Patiño-Saucedo, A., Domínguez-Morales, J.P., Rostro-González, H., Pérez-Peña, F.: Neuromorphic adaptive spiking CPG towards bio-inspired locomotion. Neurocomputing **502**, 57–70 (2022). https://doi.org/10.1016/j.neucom.2022.06.085
12. Luo, J., Ye, S., Su, J., Jin, B.: Prismatic quasi-direct-drives for dynamic quadruped locomotion with high payload capacity. Int. J. Mech. Sci. **235**, 107698 (2022). https://doi.org/10.1016/j.ijmecsci.2022.107698
13. Ji, Q., et al.: Synthesizing the optimal gait of a quadruped robot with soft actuators using deep reinforcement learning. Robot. Comput. Integr. Manuf. **78**, 107698 (2022). https://doi.org/10.1016/j.rcim.2022.102382
14. Quigley, M.: ROS: an open-source robot operating system. Paper presented at the ICRA workshop on open source software, January 2009
15. Koenig, N., Howard, A.: Design and use paradigms for gazebo, an open-source multi-robot simulator (2004). Paper presented at the 2004 IEEE/RSJ international conference on intelligent robots and systems (IROS) (IEEE Cat. No.04CH37566), Sendai, Japan, 28 September–02 October 2004 (2004)

16. Fuentes, J.C.: Generador de modos de caminado para robot cuadrúpedo basado en principios neurofisiológicos (2006). Work Presented like Master Science Thesis to Universidad Simón Bolívar(2006)

17. Cappelletto, J., Estevez, P., Grieco, J.C., Medina-Melendez, W., Fernandez-Lopez, G.: Gait synthesis in legged robot locomotion using a CPG based model, pp. 227–246 (2007)

18. Bower, J.M., Beeman, D. (eds.):The book of Genesis (2003)

19. Rico, E.M., Hernandez-Riveros, J., ARico, E.M., Hernandez, J.A.: Analysis and application of a displacement CPG-based method on articulated frames. In: Solano, A., Ordoñez, H. (eds.) Advances in Computing, CCC 2017. CCIS, vol. 735. Springer, Cham (2017). https://doi.org/10.1007/978-3-319-66562-7_36

20. Rico Mesa, E.M., Hernández-Riveros, J.A.: Modulation of central pattern generators (CPG) for the locomotion planning of an articulated robot. In: Florez, H., Diaz, C., Chavarriaga, J. (eds.) Applied Informatics, ICAI 2018. CCIS, vol. 942. Springer, Cham (2018). https://doi.org/10.1007/978-3-030-01535-0_24

21. Rico Mesa, E.M., Hernández-Riveros, J.A.: Determination of the central pattern generator parameters by a neuro-fuzzy evolutionary algorithm. In: Botto-Tobar, M., León-Acurio, J., Díaz Cadena, A., Montiel Díaz, P. (eds.) Advances in Emerging Trends and Technologies, ICAETT 2019. AISC, vol. 1066. Springer, Cham (2020). https://doi.org/10.1007/978-3-030-32022-5_48

22. Rico Mesa, E.M., Hernández-Riveros, J.-A.: Handling the transition in the locomotion of an articulated quadruped robot by adaptive CPG. IAENG **47**(4), 792–804 (2020)

23. Klir, G.J., Yuan, B.: Fuzzy Sets and Fuzzy Logic: Theory and Applications. Prentice Hall, New Jersey (1995)

24. Jaekel, J., Mikut, R., Bretthauer, G.: Fuzzy Control Systemsvol, vol. XVII. Eolss, Oxford (2004)

Brain-Computer Interfaces

Comparison of Visual and Kinesthetic Motor Imagery for Upper Limb Activity

Martha-Rocio Torres-Narváez⑩, Oliver Müller⑩,
and Alvaro David Orjuela-Cañon(✉) ⑩

School of Medicine and Health Sciences, Universidad del Rosario, Bogotá D.C., Colombia
alvaro.orjuela@urosario.edu.co

Abstract. Brain computer interfaces have different applications, according to the input stimulation of the participants and the context where they are put to use. Motor imagery is one of the most common applications. However, this specific implementation is often associated with visual imagination of the activity under study. The present proposal deals additionally with kinesthetic imagination, which includes proprioceptive sensations. For this purpose, power spectral density was computed for visual and kinesthetic motor imagery and actual movement execution. The data was compared between the three motor tasks, employing the Wilcoxon, Kruskal-Wallis, and Mann-Whitney statistic tests. Results showed a reduced dispersion of power spectral density during imagery. In addition, there were no statistically significant differences among imagery and actual movement execution.

Keyword: BCI; Motor Imagery · Kinesthetic Imagery · Rehabilitation

1 Introduction

Brain-computer interfaces (BCI) are based on electroencephalographic (EEG) recordings during mental tasks inside the experimental context. Most studies have reported the relevance of mu/alpha (8–13 Hz) and beta (14–30 Hz) bands as the primary source of cerebral information for sensorimotor tasks [1, 2]. Motor imagery (MI) is the mental imagery of an activity without the actual execution of the movement and is accessible through the recording of EEG signals during this imagination process. Due to this, different applications in the rehabilitation field are support in assistive technology design, plasticity recovery, motor learning and control of prosthetic devices, among others. Examples of this are post-stroke applications [3], and devices controlled by BCIs [4, 5].

For the MI pipeline, the EEG signal is passed through digital signal processing and analyzed based on the computation of features in the frequency domain. One of the most common techniques is to calculate the power spectral density (PSD), where EEG data originating in the primary motor cortex (electrodes C3, C4, and Cz, mainly) are processed and decoded for BCI systems [6–8].

The most common experimental conditions for the BCI approaches are visual motor imagery (VMI) and its corresponding motor execution (ME). In the former, the task for the participant is to visualize or imagine the movement under study, commonly in upper limbs. Most of the time participants can practice the task to improve. However, using kinesthetic motor imagery (KMI) can contribute to a better understanding of the mental process associated with motor activities in the brain [9]. This process considers the proprioception, which the subject feels during ME and evokes during the imagination process, and is more closely related to real perception and action [10].

In spite of the different studies, VMI has been widely employed with BCIs. Nevertheless, the KMI strategy has become more used due to the possibility of measuring the difficulty for user's performance. In addition, its complexity can be analyzed in this kind of tasks associated with a more complete mental approach. For control or rehabilitation, the KMI approach is preferable because of its relation to learning and brain plasticity [11, 12]. In recent years, research on KMI has increased with an orientation to answer questions associated to intra- and intervariability for the participants, variation in quality, and BCI performance [13]. Other studies have focused on aspects beyond physiological characteristics, such as acceptability, emotional state, and motivation of BCI users [14, 15]. Furthermore, there are various fields of interest to experiment and solve questions regarding these topics.

One study compared the VMI and KMI approaches in the control of robotic arms, finding that identification of the hand used in imagery based on EEG data was more successful for KMI during imagery practice, but a statistically significant effect occurred only for the right hand and one of four blocks of training. When in a second phase imagery was used to control the robotic arm, identification of the hand used in imagery showed a tendency to be more successful for VMI, but this was not statistically significant [16]. Another study used functional magnetic resonance imaging to explore the brain areas active during VMI and KMI in order to inform the use of these modalities for BCIs. The results showed common activation in the left premotor area and the inferior parietal lobule, whereas there was stronger activation for KMI in the supplementary motor area and insula [17].

The objective of the present work is to compare the different modes of motor imagery in an experimental task for a right upper limb movement. For this purpose, an analysis based on power spectral density was done for the three scenarios: i) VMI, ii) KMI, and iii) ME.

2   Methodology

2.1   Database

A group of 40 healthy participants was recruited for the present study (7 males and 33 females, with an average age of 23.5 ± 7.2 years). The group was considered according to age, availability, and volunteering in the experimental design. The ethical committee approval was followed through document DVO005 1066-CV1180, according to the WMA Declaration of Helsinki. All participants signed an informed consent document. The subjects did not report a critical medical history regarding neural, antidepressant or neurological treatments. In addition, the group did not report consumption of coffee or other stimulant substances.

EEG signals were acquired using an Electrical Geodesics Inc. (EGI) setup with 32 channels, a sampling frequency of 500 samples per second and Cz as reference. Data acquisition occurred with the EGI Net Station software and data processing with the MNE Python library [18].

2.2 Experimental Protocol

The movement was grabbing a ball placed on a table with the right hand and moving it up above the head. The participants had to either visualize the movement (VMI), feel the movement in a kinesthetic mode (KMI), or execute the movement (ME) forty times during acquisition. The movement and the three task modes were explained to and practiced with the participants before the experiment. Each participant received a random sequence of trials in the three modes, in order to avoid repetition effects.

Figure 1 visualizes the block diagram of the trial timeline. The present analysis includes a comparison between the baseline, marked as "*Lin+*", and the beginning of the task related to the "*ini+*" mark, associated to any of the VMI, KMI, and ME activities. According to the protocol, a period of two seconds after the initial mark was used for the baseline and a time segment of four seconds for the MI task.

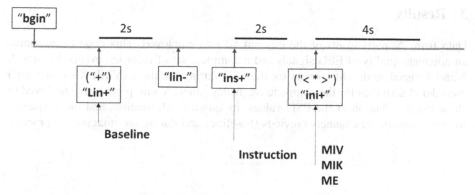

Fig. 1. Timeline for the experimentation

2.3 Signal Processing

An inspection of the signals was done to discard those data that had uncommon behavior related to atypical values in the amplitude. In addition, it was checked whether the tasks were completed for all considered activities. The present work considered the baseline (previous) and activity (during) segments aforementioned. The channels C3 and C4 over the sensorimotor cortex regions were chosen for analysis as the EEG signal from these sensors captures motor activity [7, 19]. Then, a first filtering process based on a Butterworth filter with a bandwidth between 0.5 and 60 Hz and tenth order was implemented, according to previously reported analyses [20]. This process allows removing artifacts of low and high frequencies. A second filter was applied to extract in an independent manner the alpha (8 to 13 Hz) and beta (14 to 30 Hz) bands associated with BCI and MI systems [1, 5].

Filtered signals were subjected to the PSD computation, taking as a baseline the fixation interval named in this study as 'pre' and the interval when the imagery activity was executed, named 'pos'. The PSD was taken following different studies that have shown the advantages of this technique [21, 22]. Normalization was carried out based on the PSD for all measurements, with the objective to have a weighted value that has more significance. The Welch algorithm was used to compute the PSD, which calculates the spectral power in subsegments of one second with an overlapping of 0.5 s [23, 24].

Three scenarios were computed based on the acquired signals and the three experimental approaches: MIV, MIK, and ME. For this purpose, a comparison between the PSD before the mental task and during the imagery/execution phase were carried out through the Wilcoxon statistical test for paired samples. In addition, the Kruskal-Wallis (KW) test was employed to determine differences between the intervals of the PSD obtained values for *pre* and *pos* data, looking for differences between the considered approaches. Finally, the Mann-Whitney (MW) test was used to compare unpaired samples between the MIV, KMI, and ME activities [25]. All tests were nonparametric, in order to avoid restrictions regarding the data distributions.

3   Results

Data from 26 participants of the original 40 was employed. This done to guarantee an adequate quality of EEG signals and a complete set of recorded events. Figures 2, 3 and 4 visualize the differences for the PSD during the three (VMI, KMI, and ME) considered activities for the complete frequency range. Violin plots were employed to show the distribution of the PSD values, its quartile information, and the frequency for both considered channels previous (baseline) and during the imagination process.

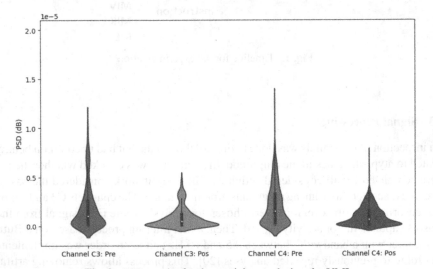

Fig. 2. PSD results for the participants during the VMI

Information from the C3 and C4 channels is displayed simultaneously to observe the effect of this measure side by side. In addition, Figs. 5, 6 and 7 exhibit the results for the PSD after the filtering process for obtaining the alpha and beta band information (the upper part shows the alpha band, and the bottom part the beta band).

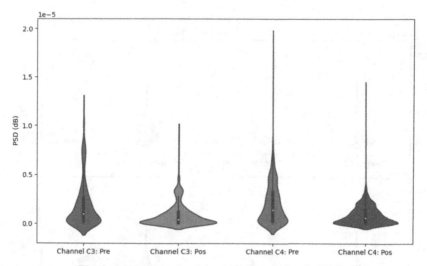

Fig. 3. PSD results for the participants during the KMI.

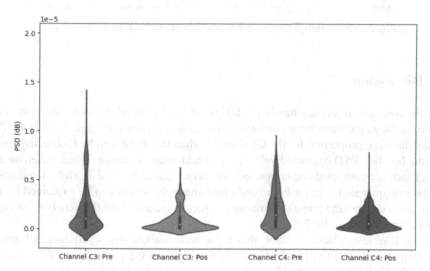

Fig. 4. PSD results for the participants during the ME.

Table 1 shows the *p-values* for the Wilcoxon test, where the hypothesis that the data populations underlying the samples, for *pre* and *pos* segments, have the same location is rejected. Table 2 presents the results of the Kruskal-Wallis hypothesis test that compares the interval of the PSD values for all *pre* and all *pos* independently, in a similar fashion as an *ANOVA*, but in a nonparametric mode. Finally, Tables 3 and 4 show the *p*-values for the MW test, comparing the PSD for unpaired values between the VMI, KMI, and ME modes. In this way, it is possible to validate the visual information provided by the violin plots.

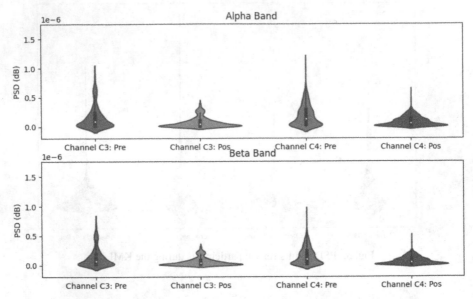

Fig. 5. PSD results for alpha and beta bands during task associated to VMI.

4   Discussion

For the complete frequency band (0.5–60 Hz), the C3 channel shows a reduction in the interquartile range when the imagination process is occurring (see Figs. 2, 3 and 4). This is not the same proportion for the C4 channel when the dispersion had more dispersion for the baseline PSD computed values. This phenomenon changes when the alpha and beta bands are computed and compared similarly. Figures 5, 6 and 7 exhibit a reduction in the interquartile range for both bands and channels, which can be explained by the analysis in the specific range of frequency values associated with the beta band as other works have reported [19, 20].

The KW tests (Table 2) show that there were statistically significant differences between the three activities (VMI, KMI, and ME) in the *pre* and *pos* EEG signals (Table 2). The Wilcoxon tests (Table 1) determined that the PSD in *pre* and *pos* differed in a statistically significant way (Table 1) and that this was the case for C3 and C4, the different frequency bands, and the activity modes. The MW analysis (Tables 3 and 4) shows that there were no differences for the comparisons between the activities. The statistical results manifest how the experimentation can be analyzed in a complementary mode beyond the observation of PSD value dispersion. These tests show how the

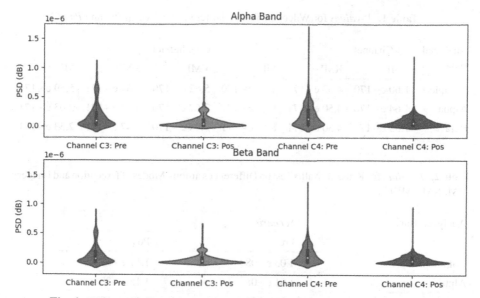

Fig. 6. PSD results for alpha and beta bands during the task associated to KMI.

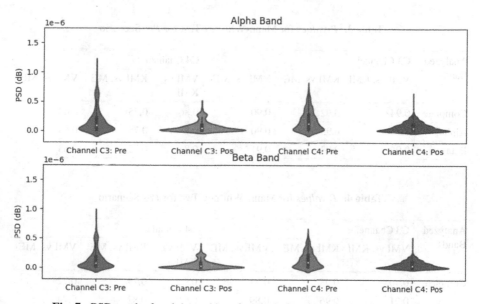

Fig. 7. PSD results for alpha and beta bands during the task associated to ME.

PSD changed when the imagery process was happening, with values that are more concentrated. Despite the observed differences in the Wilcoxon for *pre* and *pos* analysis, the MW test values allowed to reject the null hypothesis about medians for the three

Table 1. *P-values* for Wilcoxon Test on Differences between *Pre* and *Pos*

Analyzed Bands	C3 Channel			C4 Channel		
	VMI	KMI	ME	VMI	KMI	ME
Complete	1.60 e−170	4.33 e−171	1.57 e−170	5.62 e−170	2.64 e−171	5.59 e−171
Alpha	1.64 e−170	4.50 e−171	9.13 e−171	3.67 e−170	3.20 e−171	3.03 e−171
Beta	1.53 e−170	4.30 e−171	8.57 e−171	3.44 e−170	2.47 e−171	2.33 e−171

Table 2. *P-values* for Kruskal-Wallis Test on Differences among Modes of Execution and Imagery (VM, KMI, ME)

Analyzed Bands	*Scenario*	
	Pre	Pos
Complete	1.03 e−08	1.17 e−08
Alpha	1.01 e−08	1.15 e−08
Beta	1.01 e−08	1.14 e−08

Table 3. *P-values* for Mann-Whitney Test for *Pre* Scenario

Analyzed Bands	C3 Channel			C4 Channel		
	VMI vs. KMI	KMI vs. ME	VMI vs. ME	VMI vs. KMI	KMI vs. ME	VMI vs. ME
Complete	0.94	0.92	0.90	0.86	0.75	0.63
Alpha	0.95	0.93	0.90	0.86	0.75	0.63
Beta	0.95	0.93	0.91	0.86	0.75	0.63

Table 4. *P-values* for Mann-Whitney Test for *Pos* Scenario

Analyzed Bands	C3 Channel			C4 Channel		
	VMI vs. KMI	KMI vs. ME	VMI vs. ME	VMI vs. KMI	KMI vs. ME	VMI vs. ME
Complete	0.90	0.98	0.91	0.92	0.79	0.72
Alpha	0.91	0.96	0.89	0.91	0.82	0.74
Beta	0.91	0.96	0.89	0.92	0.81	0.74

approaches are the same. In addition, similar analyses based on statistical tests to support the use of the PSD computation have been explored to discriminate the EEG signals [23, 25, 26].

Limitations of the present study are associated with the number of participants employed for the analysis, which is preferable to be higher to support better statistical results. The analysis of one activity of the right upper limbs can be considered as a limitation compared to current options that consider lower, both limbs or different movements [27]. However, the study of the EEG signals for VMI compared to KMI offered a different paradigm reported than in most of the BCI literature. Despite these aspects, the present proposal exhibits preliminary results that can be exploited to find more relevant information about BCI and the kinesthetic approach.

5 Conclusion

The present proposal for comparison of the VMI and KMI approaches was analyzed through the employment of PSD computation on EEG signals. The dispersion of PSD values shows the effect of the MI task on the *pos* interval. However, the used statistical tests did not evidence differences between the two imagery approaches or ME.

These results contribute to the understanding of how the analysis of kinesthetic MI in a parallel mode to the visual one can provide more information about the relevance of developing a complete experimentation of BCI scenarios that can be transfer in clinical or sport settings.

Acknowledgment. The authors acknowledge the support of the Universidad del Rosario for funding this project: IV-FCS023 In addition, the contribution of research incubator team *Semillero en Inteligencia Artificial en Salud: Semill-IAS and Rehabilitation Sciences and Behavioral Sciences Research Groups*.

References

1. Rimbert, S., Bougrain, L., Fleck, S.: Learning how to generate kinesthetic motor imagery using a BCI-based learning environment: a comparative study based on guided or trial-and-error approaches. In: Proceedings of the 2020 IEEE International Conference on Systems, Man, and Cybernetics (SMC), pp. 2483–2498 (2020)
2. Pfurtscheller, G., Da Silva, F.H.L.: Event-related EEG/MEG synchronization and desynchronization: basic principles. Clin. Neurophysiol. **110**, 1842–1857 (1999)
3. Cervera, M.A., et al.: Brain-computer interfaces for post-stroke motor rehabilitation: a meta-analysis. Ann. Clin. Transl. Neurol. **5**, 651–663 (2018)
4. Mane, R., Chouhan, T., Guan, C.: BCI for stroke rehabilitation: motor and beyond. J. Neural Eng. **17**, 41001 (2020)
5. Robinson, N., Mane, R., Chouhan, T., Guan, C.: Emerging trends in BCI-robotics for motor control and rehabilitation. Curr. Opin. Biomed. Eng. **20**, 100354 (2021)
6. Antelis, J.M., Gudiño-Mendoza, B., Falcón, L.E., Sanchez-Ante, G., Sossa, H.: Dendrite morphological neural networks for motor task recognition from electroencephalographic signals. Biomed. Signal Process. Control **44**, 12–24 (2018)
7. Hernández-Rojas, L.G., Montoya, O.M., Antelis, J.M.: Anticipatory detection of self-paced rehabilitative movements in the same upper limb from EEG signals. IEEE Access **8**, 119728–119743 (2020)

8. Triana Guzmán, N., Orjuela-Cañón, Á.D., Jutinico Alarcon, A.L.: Incremental training of neural network for motor tasks recognition based on brain-computer interface. In: Nyström, I., Hernández Heredia, Y., Milián Núñez, V. (eds.) Progress in Pattern Recognition, Image Analysis, Computer Vision, and Applications. CIARP 2019. LNCS, vol. 11896, pp. 610–619. Springer, Cham (2019). https://doi.org/10.1007/978-3-030-33904-3_57

9. Neuper, C., Scherer, R., Reiner, M., Pfurtscheller, G.: Imagery of motor actions: differential effects of kinesthetic and visual–motor mode of imagery in single-trial EEG. Cogn. Brain Res. **25**, 668–677 (2005). https://doi.org/10.1016/j.cogbrainres.2005.08.014

10. Guillot, A., Collet, C., Nguyen, V.A., Malouin, F., Richards, C., Doyon, J.: Brain activity during visual versus kinesthetic imagery: an fMRI study. Hum. Brain Mapp. **30**, 2157–2172 (2009)

11. Rimbert, S., Fleck, S.: Long-term kinesthetic motor imagery practice with a BCI: Impacts on user experience, motor cortex oscillations and BCI performances. Comput. Human Behav. **146**, 107789 (2023)

12. Jeunet, C., Lotte, F., n'Kaoua, B.: Human learning for brain–computer interfaces. In: Brain–Computer Interfaces 1 Found. Methods, pp. 233–250 (2016)

13. Saha, S., Baumert, M.: Intra-and inter-subject variability in EEG-based sensorimotor brain computer interface: a review. Front. Comput. Neurosci. **13**, 87 (2020)

14. Alimardani, M., Gherman, D.-E.: Individual differences in motor imagery BCIS: a study of gender, mental states and mu suppression. In: Proceedings of the 2022 10th International Winter Conference on Brain-Computer Interface (BCI), pp. 1–7 (2022)

15. Škola, F., Tinková, S., Liarokapis, F.: Progressive training for motor imagery brain-computer interfaces using gamification and virtual reality embodiment. Front. Hum. Neurosci. **13**, 329 (2019)

16. Arfaras, G., et al.: Visual versus kinesthetic motor imagery for BCI control of robotic arms (Mercury 2.0). In: Proceedings of the 2017 IEEE 30th International Symposium on Computer-Based Medical Systems (CBMS), pp. 440–445 (2017)

17. Lee, W.H., et al.: Target-oriented motor imagery for grasping action: different characteristics of brain activation between kinesthetic and visual imagery. Sci. Rep. **9**, 12770 (2019)

18. Gramfort, A., et al.: MEG and EEG data analysis with MNE-Python. Front. Neurosci. **7**, 1–13 (2013). https://doi.org/10.3389/fnins.2013.00267

19. Gudiño-Mendoza, B., Sánchez-Ante, G., Antelis, J.M.: Detecting the intention to move upper limbs from electroencephalographic brain signals. Comput. Math. Methods Med. **2016**, 3195373:1–3195373:11 (2016). https://doi.org/10.1155/2016/3195373

20. Orjuela-Cañón, A.D., Renteria-Meza, O., Hernández, L.G., Ruíz-Olaya, A.F., Cerquera, A., Antelis, J.M.: Self-organizing maps for motor tasks recognition from electrical brain signals. In: Mendoza, M., Velastín, S. (eds.) Progress in Pattern Recognition, Image Analysis, Computer Vision, and Applications. CIARP 2017. LNCS, vol. 10657, pp. 458–465. Springer, Cham (2018). https://doi.org/10.1007/978-3-319-75193-1_55. ISBN 9783319751924

21. Alam, M.N., Ibrahimy, M.I., Motakabber, S.M.A.: Feature extraction of EEG signal by power spectral density for motor imagery based BCI. In: Proceedings of the 2021 8th International Conference on Computer and Communication Engineering (ICCCE), pp. 234–237 (2021)

22. Kim, C., Sun, J., Liu, D., Wang, Q., Paek, S.: An effective feature extraction method by power spectral density of EEG signal for 2-class motor imagery-based BCI. Med. Biol. Eng. Comput. **56**, 1645–1658 (2018)

23. Yu, X., Aziz, M.Z., Hou, Y., Li, H., Lv, J., Jamil, M.: An extended computer aided diagnosis system for robust BCI applications. In: Proceedings of the 2021 IEEE 9th International Conference on Information, Communication and Networks (ICICN), pp. 475–480 (2021)

24. Gupta, A., et al.: On the utility of power spectral techniques with feature selection techniques for effective mental task classification in noninvasive BCI. IEEE Trans. Syst. Man, Cybern. Syst. **51**, 3080–3092 (2019)

25. Yu, X., Aziz, M.Z., Sadiq, M.T., Fan, Z., Xiao, G.: A new framework for automatic detection of motor and mental imagery EEG signals for robust BCI systems. IEEE Trans. Instrum. Meas. **70**, 1–12 (2021)
26. Yang, Y.J., Jeon, E.J., Kim, J.S., Chung, C.K.: Characterization of kinesthetic motor imagery compared with visual motor imageries. Sci. Rep. **11**, 3751 (2021)
27. Triana-Guzman, N., Orjuela-Cañon, A.D., Jutinico, A.L., Mendoza-Montoya, O., Antelis, J.M.: Decoding EEG rhythms offline and online during motor imagery for standing and sitting based on a brain-computer interface. Front. Neuroinform. (2022)

Effect of an Imagery Training on Biomechanical Aspects of a Sport Skill in Gymnasts of the Met Chia Club

Lina María Estefanía Guzmán Riaño(✉) ⓘ, Erica Mabel Mancera Soto ⓘ,
and Gustavo Adolfo Pineda Ortiz ⓘ

Physiology Department, Universidad Nacional de Colombia, Bogotá, Colombia
lmguzmanr@unal.edu.co

Abstract. Introduction: Imagery and action observation allow to mentally simulate movements and therefore to train cognitive aspects of learning, memory, and motor control, however, its potential as a training tool for children is unknown. This research aimed to propose a design of imagery training, which evaluates the effect on biomechanical aspects of the execution of a basic sport skill in an early-age initiation sport, such as artistic gymnastics.

Materials and Methods: Biomechanical sensors were used to evaluate the performance of the back arch in 5 gymnasts between the ages of 7 and 12, in addition, the skill questionnaire for imagery in sport (CHID) and the Children's Movement Imagery Questionnaire (MIQ-3) were applied. Subsequently, a training of 14 sessions of imagery was performed, varying its difficulty and specificity. A post-intervention evaluation was also carried out.

Results: Suggest that imagery was effective for improving aspects of movement performance, such as coordination and propulsion,

Conclusions: The improvement, according to the theory of Berstein dynamic systems, is an indicator of learning and motor control over the back arch. However, the study's limitations in terms of sample size should be borne in mind.

Keywords: Imagery · Artistic gymnastics · Motor learning · Motor control · Biomechanics

1 Introduction

The training of cognitive processes is fundamental in any sports practice. It manages to enhance the performance of the athlete through the use of intervention techniques, such as Imagery (IM) and Action Observation (AO), which train memory and procedural (motor) learning of sports skills [1]. The AO is a mental simulation technique that consists of observing a movement either live or in a video recording [2]. In this way, this visual stimulation promotes the activation of neural networks associated with the brain's representation of the observed movement, mainly in sensory, perceptual, and affective characteristics, making it a bottom-up processing [3]. On the other hand, IM is the ability to create vivid mental representations or images, which can be controlled and

© The Author(s), under exclusive license to Springer Nature Switzerland AG 2024
J. A. Riascos Salas et al. (Eds.): LAWCN 2023, CCIS 2108, pp. 106–117, 2024.
https://doi.org/10.1007/978-3-031-63848-0_8

maintained over time [4]. This allows the subject to mentally experience the performance or observation of motor actions [1, 2] by consciously recovering the motor skill (mental representation) from long-term memory, which turns imagery into top-down processing [2, 3].

These techniques are based on the hierarchical theories of motor control, such as the theory of dynamic systems proposed by Nicolai Berstein [5], which states that the central nervous system is responsible for generating higher-level orders (generate action), in the motor cortex. Commands are sent to lower levels such as the spinal cord, muscles, and articulations [6], or what Berstein calls synergies [5]. In this manner, motor learning is understood as the process by which our experience gradually modifies the central nervous system (CNS) [6, 7 (81–82)] through what is known as synaptic plasticity, evidenced in the execution of a motor skill that, for Bernstein, is the domain of the Redundant Degrees of Freedom (DF) [8].

It has been investigated how these mental training techniques can improve the learning of sports skills, measured by changes observed by experienced judges [9, 10], which found an improvement not only in the execution but also in the ability to evaluate their performance and others [9]. However, there is a difference between experts and novices, especially in the effect of imagery training, in short duration [10]. Additionally, mental training studies have been conducted that evaluate performance using biomechanical analysis techniques, finding an improvement in performance in biomechanical parameters such as flight height, contact time with the ground, verticality, bending and extension angles [11, 12]. Also, it has been studied the AO and IM training together improve the ability to generate images [13], and that adding a feedback session with proprioceptive information can improve the ability to generate kinesthetic mental images [14].

However, imagery training is usually directed mainly at adolescents and adults. Although some authors have highlighted the importance of investigating the effects of imagery mental training at early developmental ages, because it is a critical period of physiological and psychological development for learning basic motor skills, they are fundamental to perform more complex ones [9, 15, 16]. Even so, other authors say that it is necessary to bear in mind, this population is in a stage of brain and cognitive development that can limit the ability to generate mental representations and adequate motor planning of the sports skill [16]. Therefore, studies have been conducted in children [15] that demonstrated an IM and AO training is effective to improve performance of a basic motor skill. However, in child athletes imagery training has not been proposed especially for this population, which means the possibility of adapting the imagery to the physiological and cognitive development of child athletes to train complex motor skills and the effect that this training can have on the improvement on the execution and learning of sports skills is unknown.

The need to address this problem, particularly in children athletes, lies in the fact that in recent years, the practice specialized in certain sports is increasing at younger ages. This is due to the belief that this practice helps children win and achieve athletic excellence [17]. One example is artistic gymnastics, a discipline of precision [18] characterized by a series of routines in different apparatus (vault, beam, bars, floor).

Therefore, IM training has been proposed for girls aged 7 to 12 to improve an elemental skill in artistic gymnastics. To evaluate the effect of this technique on biomechanical aspects of performance, specifically change in intra- and inter-joint coordination and propulsion of lower limbs.

2   Methods

2.1   Ethical Considerations

This study has the approval of the Ethics Committee of the Faculty of Sciences of the Universidad Nacional de Colombia.

2.2   Participants

Originally, 7 gymnasts were part of the study. However, two participants did not complete the training and were excluded for data analysis. The final 5 gymnasts were between 7 and 12 years old (M = 9.8, SD 1.72), who practiced gymnastics for half-year to 4 years ago (M = 1.7, SD = 1.25) and trained between 4 and 8 h per week (M = 5.2, SD 1.6).

2.3   Sport Skill of Gymnastics

The maneuver of the Back Arch (see Fig. 1) [19] consists of a rotation of the body on the sagittal plane that begins with a hyperextension in the back [20] to reach the arch posture. The rotation continues by the propulsion made from the support foot, in such a way that a split handstand is reached. Then, the rotation of the lower limbs (LB) continues until contact is made with the floor. Finally, the propulsion is transferred to the hands by pushing and lifting the trunk to achieve the intended posture [21].

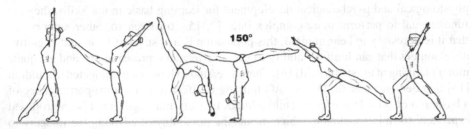

Fig. 1. Technique of the sequence of movements of the back arch. Includes the arch posture (third draw in the image) and the split handstand posture (fourth draw).

2.4   Procedure

We used a pre/post experimental design of multiple cases with an 8-phase training consisting of a physical practice guided by AO, a physical practice with kinesthetic feedback, 2 training phases in AO, and 3 training phases in IM. The complete process consisted of 17 sessions, 14 of imagery (10 face-to-face and 4 virtual), and 3 physical practice sessions guided by mental simulation techniques. During this time, the gymnasts maintained their usual physical and sports training. All participants were evaluated before the first training phase in AO and after the last training phase in IM.

Before the imagery training, 3 sessions were held, the first of presentation and familiarization with the materials, procedures, and instructions of the IM training. Then a physical practice session guided by AO of the back arch and after this session the initial evaluation was made, where gymnasts were supplied with 2 imagery ability questionnaires. Also, the participants were asked to perform the back arch while inertial sensors were placed on their hips, knees, and ankles. The imagery training began with 5 sessions of AO and IM training with an external perspective. After that, a physical kinesthetic training session and visual feedback (KS) were carried out, followed by 5 training sessions in AO and IM with internal perspectives. Then, another physical training KS was carried out to end with 4 IM training sessions. Upon completion of this training, the evaluation of the imagery ability and the back arch performance were performed again (see Fig. 2).

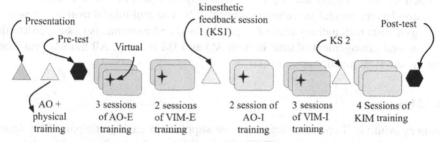

Fig. 2. Procedure of evaluations and training. The figure shows the complete intervention of 20 sessions that include sessions of action observation (AO-E) with external perspective, visual imagery with external perspective (VIM-E), action observation with internal perspective (AO-I) visual imagery with internal perspective (VIM-I), kinesthetic imagery (KI) and physical practice with kinesthetic feedback sessions (KS).

2.5 IM Training

The fundamental aspect of the IM training design is the progressive character of mental training, with the aim that gymnasts familiarize themselves and collect the necessary information to create the mental image properly during each type of imagery, and that the presentation of them was in a progressive nature according to the cognitive difficulty that it demands [22–25]. Therefore, the first part of the training consisted of a physical practice session in which gymnasts were asked to observe a video in detail of the ideal execution of a back arch from an external sagittal perspective (see Fig. 1) in order to try to execute the maneuver as similarly as possible. In this way, when they took the first sessions of AO with an external perspective, they were aware of the importance of detailing the video as if they were going to execute it later. These sessions also sought to strengthen the mental image of the movement, for the following sessions of external visual imagery (VIM-E) in which the visual guide is eliminated. However, auditory tracks at the beginning and end of the movement were maintained.

In preparation for the following sessions, a KS was held, in which the athlete was asked to perform the back arch, making her aware of what she observed and felt during the execution of each posture (see Fig. 1). Subsequently, the AO session was held with an internal perspective, in which the video of the back arch execution from an internal perspective was given to form a visual guide of what is seen when properly performing the back arch and to build a mental image in the following sessions of internal visual imagery (VIM-I), in which any visual stimulus is eliminated. However, auditory tracks at the beginning and end of the movement were maintained.

Finally, in preparation for the last phase of kinesthetic imagery training (KIM), a KS was held where the athlete had to perform the back arch being aware of the kinesthetic sensations they perceived, such as tension, extension, impulse, and displacement of the body segments after that the KIM was held where the gymnasts create a mental image of the back arch that include those sensations. This was with any visual stimulus, but auditory tracks at the beginning and end of the movement were maintained.

Each training session lasted 5 min, consisting of 5 sets of 7 trials. Each one was understood as the mental execution of a back arch. The multimedia material presented to the gymnasts had auditory cues of beginning and end movements to standardize the duration and management of time in both AO and IM training. All training was done after the physical practice of gymnasts.

2.6 Measures

Imagery Ability. Two questionnaires were supplied to each participant: The Sports Imagery Ability Questionnaire (CHID) [26], which evaluates the imagery ability of different sports-related content, through 12 items, which corresponds to 4 subscales: Strategy, Skill, Affective, and Objectives, and the Movement Imagery Questionnaire (MIQ-3). Which evaluates the ability to properly visualize all four movements using internal visual imagery, external visual imagery, and kinesthetic imagery [25].

Execution. The movement was recorded using 6 inertial sensors (Xsens dot) on the hips, knees, and ankles. This device is equipped with a 3D rate gyroscope that can be used to estimate orientation by the numerical integration of the rate turn, a 3D accelerometer that can be used as a stabilization reference by tracking the linear acceleration, and a 3D magnetometer that can establish the orientation in space by sensing the strength and direction of the surrounding magnetic field [27]. To track the movement this output is processed by two algorithms the Strap-Down Integration (SDI) that integrates the measurements of the gyroscope and accelerometer and increments at a lower rate of 60 Hz or 120 Hz and the Xsens Kalman Filter (XKF) Core that uses de SDI and magnetometer data to produces accurate estimates of orientation and free acceleration in real-time. The inertial and orientation data are then either transmitted to an external device via the on-board BLE module or stored locally in the memory (for more specifications, see Acala et al. [27]).

Coordination was evaluated by inter-joint coordination from a multivariate app-roach (PCA), in which 3 indicators were obtained: global coordination (sagittal plane),

3D coordination (in all axes of the movement), and coordination of LB. Since complex coordination patterns involve kinematics dependencies or joint kinematics varying at the same rate of flexion/extension, statistical covariance may be a potential descriptor of inter-segmental coordination. Principal component analysis (PCA) relies on reducing multiplanar kinematic components per joint (flexion, extension, rotation times series) depicted by every angular displacement of the sensor (pitch, roll, and yaw around X, Y, Z axis respectively) in a few numbers of components (embedded time series) and summarizing all of those kinematic patterns. The number of components, as the experimental parameter, may represent an overall coordinate measurement since fewer components imply a reduction of joint displacement "out of plane", increasing "in plane" covariation (jointly flexion or jointly extension), and capturing higher variance of the original set (cumulative variance). Being kinematic coordination is also a temporal phenomenon, phase shift (time differences between maximal joint flexion) is computed.

Propulsion was evaluated by intra-joint coordination of LB was assessed separately by the angular displacement and angular velocity relationship because jerky and high-speed motions involved in foot take-off and pushing off ground may be captured by a wider area over a two-dimensional plane.

Statical Analysis. A T-student test was carried out for related samples or a Wilcoxon sign ranges test, depending on the fulfillment of assumptions of normality of each indicator, to estimate the effect of imagery training.

3   Results

3.1   Coordination

Before and after the training, the inter-joint coordination showed in all the participants a mastery of the redundant degrees of freedom. In the articulation-articulation graph (see Fig. 3) it is possible to see a cyclic and regular representation in each trial, generating a coordinated and stable pattern in the execution of the back arch. Which is characterized

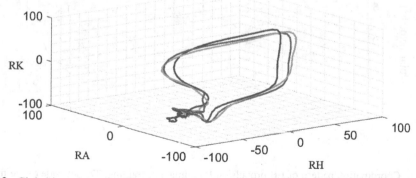

Fig. 3. Global inter-joint coordination of rights LB in each trial of the execution. The joint-joint graph shows the PCA indicator for the right knee (RK), right ankle (RA), right hip (RH).

by asynchronous phases of displacement that can be observed in the flat parts of the curve, which have a sagittal component by the hip displacement, one longitudinal by the ankle displacement that occurs at the ends of the loop, and a coronal component by the displacement of the knee that occurs synchronously to the ankle. From this form we found changes in the 3D coordination indicator, which evaluated the execution in the 3 planes of the movement, going from 72.7% (SD = −4.97) before the training to 76.7% (SD = −2.51) after it, which represented a significant change (p = 0.036). However, there were no significant changes in the LB coordination or in the global coordination.

3.2 Propulsion

Figure 4 shows the coordination pattern in the form of loops, generated by each joint. It was found that the propulsion carried out by all the joints of the right hemibody had

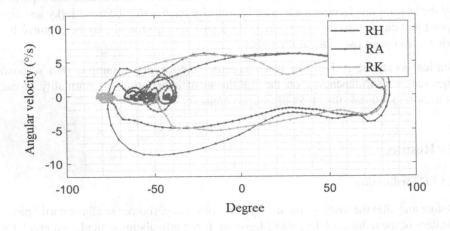

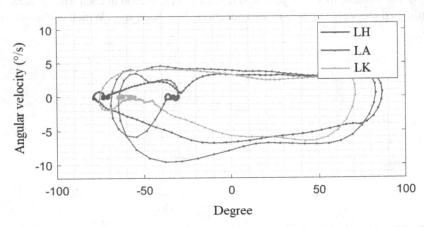

Fig. 4. Coordination pattern of LB propulsion Post-imagery training. The left side of the figure shows the phase plane of the right hip (RH), right ankle (RA), and right knee (RK). The right side of the figure shows the phase plane of the left hip (LH), left ankle (LA), and left knee (LK).

significant changes after the imagery training (see Fig. 5), specifically in the first trial knee sensor (p = 0.04, see row 5 of Table 1), second trial knee sensor (p = 0.00, see row 6 Table 1) and mean of all trials knee sensor (p = 0.01, see row 8 Table 1), second trial hip sensor (p = 0.05, see row 2 Table 1), second trial ankle sensor (p = 0.03, see row 10 Table 1), third trial ankle sensor (p = 0.01, sew row 11 Table 1) and mean of all trials ankle sensor (p = 0.00, see row 12 Table 1). While in the left hemibody significant differences occurred only in the second trial ankle sensor (p = 0.01).

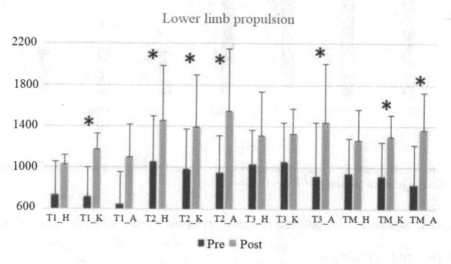

Fig. 5. The bar chart of right LB propulsion pre- and post-training in IM. Values for the inter-joint coordination indicator are shown in all trials (E) for each joint, hip (H), knee (K), and ankle (A), and the mean of trials (M) for each joint. Significant differences (*) between pre-training and post-training assessment are noted.

3.3 IM Ability

Two subscales of the MIQ-3 questionnaire showed significant differences after training (see Fig. 6), the subscale of IK (Mpre = 5.4, Mpost = 6.4, p = 0.04) and the external imagery (Mpre = 5.8, Mpost = 6.7 p = 0.00) while in the CHID questionnaire, no changes were significant.

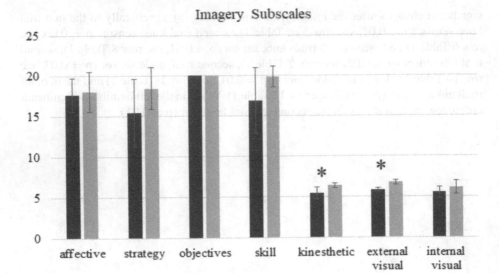

Fig. 6. The bar chart of the imagery subscales scores pre- and post-training in IM. The significant difference between pre-and post-scores is shown (*).

Table 1. Significance of the difference between right propulsion before and after imagery sessions

Right Joint	Trial	Propulsion					
		Pre-IM	SD/IQR	Post-IM	SD/IQR	diff.	p-value
Hip	1	736,67	320,15	1029,30	89,09	292,63	0,14
	2*	1056,54	442,16	1459,71	528,81	403,17	**0,05***
	3	1192,52	861,42–1319,36	1129,63	1010,37–1533,42	−62,89	0,16
	mean	1075,69	935,21–1140,1	1214,12	1184,31–1412,82	138,43	0,06
Knee	1*	713,16	292,00	1175,12	155,13	461,96	**0,04***
	2*	1187,52	987,5349–1243,32	1548,04	1288,63–1705,44	360,52	**0,00***
	3	1054,74	380,95	1333,34	237,85	278,60	0,07
	mean	916,69	332,24	1300,00	208,52	383,31	**0,01***
Ankle	1	643,13	317,92	1100,12	319,84	456,99	0,08
	2*	952,78	357,89	1544,37	606,16	591,59	**0,03***
	3*	912,76	520,81	1438,55	563,66	525,79	**0,01***
	mean*	836,23	378,73	1361,02	364,24	524,79	**0,00***

The standard deviation (SD) was calculated for the variables with a normal distribution, for the others the interquartile range (IQR) was calculated. *$p \leq 0.5$

4 Discussion

Childhood is the period in which there is great potential for biological and physiological development of motor control [15]. So, the training of physical and mental skills at this stage of development is fundamental. However, while the scientific advance in the mental training of motor learning in children is limited, this raises the question, of whether a child between 7 and 12 years old would benefit from these techniques. Based on the study, it was found that progressive IM training, with a motor approach, improves the performance of a motor skill in artistic gymnastics. Regarding efficiency indices related to coordination, the control of the DF, and the propulsion are directly related to motor learning [8].

It has been shown that IM training with AO sessions can improve the learning of basic motor skills in children [15], and complex motor skills in adolescents [13, 14]. However, the present research found that in child athletes an IM training with AO session and kinesthetic feedback session can be used to improve the performance of complex motor skills, as the back arch, which is consistent with was reported in adolescent athletes [14]. Which shows that the adding sessions overcome this limitation and allow the participants to collect kinesthetic movement information, corroborated in the present study by the finding of improvements in the ability to KI, which does not agree with what is reported in the literature which states that this is the most difficult modality to execute therefore, its applicability to children is questionable [22–25, 28]. On the other hand, the change in the ability to perform external IMV is consistent with what was reported in literature [22–25] since it is one of the easiest modalities to execute, children are able to perform it.

Also, was found difference in the execution of the back arch, regarding coordination and propulsion which is consistent with what was reported by Simonsmeier et al. [10] and by Doussoulin & Rehbein [15] where a similar design training was effective in improving the learning of a motor skill. Although the results are not conclusive on the impact of imagery on coordination due to the sample size and the lack of a control group, there are indications in the available literature that motor coordination, evaluated by biomechanical techniques, improved with an IM and AO training adapted for children.

5 Conclusions

The most impactful finding of this research is that progressive training in IM, AO, and kinesthetic feedback seems to enhance the motor learning of sports skill of artistic gymnastics in girls between 7 and 12 years of age in aspects such as coordination, propulsion, and imagery. However, these changes may not be noticeable if the appropriate evaluation methodology, such as biomechanical movement analysis and psychological questionnaires, are not chosen. For future research, it will be necessary to include techniques of objective evaluation of the cognitive and neurophysiological components of motor learning such as using EEG. One of the strengths of this research includes being one of the first studies to evaluate the effect of IM training, that includes AO and feedback sessions, on biomechanical and psychological indicators of motor learning in child athletes. This brings concrete validity to the results of the study. However, it has noticeable limitations in terms of sample size and the lack of a control group that manages to separate the effect of IM training from the effect of physical practice on motor learning of the sports skill studied. It is also important to note that the training time was short compared to other studies [9, 29]. Therefore, training with a greater number of sessions, while maintaining different levels of difficulty, would be relevant for future research. So, training with a greater number of sessions, but maintaining training levels based on the difficulty of imagery like in this research, would be relevant for future research.

Conflicts of Interest. The author states not to have any conflicts of interest.

References

1. Guillot, A., Collet, C. (eds.): The Neurophysiological Foundations of Mental and Motor Imagery. Oxford University Press, Oxford (2010). https://doi.org/10.1093/acprof:oso/978019 9546251.001.0001
2. Kim, T., Frank, C., Schack, T.: A systematic investigation of the effect of action observation training and motor imagery training on the development of mental representation structure and skill performance. Front. Hum. Neurosci. **11** (2017). https://doi.org/10.3389/fnhum.2017. 00499
3. Holmes, P., Calmels, C.: A neuroscientific review of imagery and observation use in sport. J. Mot. Behav. **40**(5), 433–445 (2008). https://doi.org/10.3200/jmbr.40.5.433-445
4. Wright, D.J., McCormick, S.A., Birks, S., Loporto, M., Holmes, P.S.: Action observation and imagery training improve the ease with which athletes can generate imagery. J. Appl. Sport Psychol. **27**(2), 156–170 (2014). https://doi.org/10.1080/10413200.2014.968294
5. Profeta, V.L., Turvey, M.T.: Bernstein's levels of movement construction: a contemporary perspective. Hum. Mov. Sci. **57**, 111–133 (2018). https://doi.org/10.1016/j.humov.2017. 11.013
6. Utley, A., Astill, S.: Instant Notes in Motor Control, Learning and Development (Instant Notes). Taylor & Francis, New York (2008)
7. Carlson, N.R.: Fisiología de la conducta – 8th edn. Pearson Education, New York (2006)
8. Newell, K.M., Liu, Y.T.: Collective variables and task constraints in movement coordination, control and skill. J. Mot. Behav. **53**, 1–27 (2020). https://doi.org/10.1080/00222895.2020.183 5799
9. Napolitano, S.: Performance improvement through motor imagery study of the case in artistic gymnastics. J. Hum. Sport Exerc. **12**(Proc2) (2017). https://doi.org/10.14198/jhse.2017.12. proc2.04
10. Simonsmeier, B.A., Frank, C., Gubelmann, H., Schneider, M.: The effects of motor imagery training on performance and mental representation of 7- to 15-year-old gymnasts of different levels of expertise. Sport Exerc. Perform. Psychol. **7**(2), 155–168 (2018). https://doi.org/10. 1037/spy0000117
11. Battaglia, C., D'Artibale, E., Fiorilli, G., et al.: Use of video observation and motor imagery on jumping performance in national rhythmic gymnastics athletes. Hum. Mov. Sci. **38**, 225–234 (2014). https://doi.org/10.1016/j.humov.2014.10.001
12. Le Naour, T., Ré, C., Bresciani, J.P.: 3D feedback and observation for motor learning: Application to the roundoff movement in gymnastics. Hum. Mov. Sci. **66**, 564–577 (2019). https:// doi.org/10.1016/j.humov.2019.06.008
13. Wright, D.J., et al.: Action observation and imagery training improve the ease with which athletes can generate imagery. J. Appl. Sport Psychol. **27**(2), 156–170 (2015)

14. Gmamdya, H., et al.: The positive impact of combining motor imagery, action observation and coach's feedback on archery accuracy of young athletes. Perceptual Motor Skills **130**(5), 2226–2248 (2023)

15. Doussoulin, A., Rehbein, L.: A imaginação motora como instrumento de treino das habilidades motoras em crianças. Motricidade **7**(3) (2011). https://doi.org/10.6063/motricidade.7(3).131

16. Dey, A., Barnsley, N., Mohan, R., McCormick, M., McAuley, J.H., Moseley, G.L.: Are children who play a sport or a musical instrument better at motor imagery than children who do not?: Figure 1. Br. J. Sports Med. **46**(13), 923–926 (2012). https://doi.org/10.1136/bjsports-2011-090525

17. Halilbašić, A., Kreso, A., Klepić, M., Jaganjac, A., Avdic, D.: The Osgood-Schlatter's Syndrome (OSD) and Involvement of Children of Young Age in Sports. J. Health Sci. (2019). https://doi.org/10.17532/jhsci.2019.894

18. Jemni, M.: Science of Gymnastics: Advanced Concepts. Taylor & Francis Group, New York (2018)

19. Fedecolgim, Federation internationale de gimnastique. Women's artistic gymnastics. Federation internationale de gimnastique (2019). https://www.gymnastics.sport/site/pages/discip lines/app-wag.php

20. Quinn, B.J.: Spine injuries in the aesthetic athlete. In: Spinal Injuries and Conditions in Young Athletes, pp. 89–97. Springer, New York (2013). https://doi.org/10.1007/978-1-4614-4753-5_9

21. Eyssartier, C., Poulet, Y., Marsan, T., et al.: Contribution of hip extension and lumbar lordosis during back walkover performed by rhythmic and woman artistic gymnasts: a preliminary study. Comput. Methods Biomech. Biomed. Eng. **23**(sup1), S101–S103 (2020). https://doi.org/10.1080/10255842.2020.1812841

22. Caeyenberghs, K., Tsoupas, J., Wilson, P.H., Smits-Engelsman, B.C.: Motor imagery development in primary school children. Dev. Neuropsychol. **34**(1), 103–121 (2009). https://doi.org/10.1080/87565640802499183

23. Fuchs, C.T., Becker, K., Austin, E., Tamplain, P.: Accuracy and vividness in motor imagery ability: differences between children and young adults. Dev. Neuropsychol. **45**(5), 297–308 (2020). https://doi.org/10.1080/87565641.2020.1788034

24. Gabbard, C.: Studying action representation in children via motor imagery. Brain Cogn. **71**(3), 234–239 (2009). https://doi.org/10.1016/j.bandc.2009.08.011

25. Martini, R., Carter, M.J., Yoxon, E., Cumming, J., Ste-Marie, D.M.: Development and validation of the Movement Imagery Questionnaire for Children (MIQ-C). Psychol. Sport Exerc. **22**, 190–201 (2016). https://doi.org/10.1016/j.psychsport.2015.08.008

26. Williams, S.E., Cumming, J.: Measuring athlete imagery ability: the sport imagery ability questionnaire. J. Sport Exerc. Psychol. **33**(3), 416–440 (2011). https://doi.org/10.1123/jsep.33.3.416

27. Alcala, E.R.D., Voerman, J.A., Konrath, J.M., Vydhyanathan, A.: Xsens DOT Wearable Sensor Platform White Paper. Movella

28. Souto, D.O., Cruz, T.K., Fontes, P.L., Batista, R.C., Haase, V.G.: Motor imagery development in children: changes in speed and accuracy with increasing age. Front. Pediatr. **8** (2020). https://doi.org/10.3389/fped.2020.00100

29. Seif-Barghi, T., Kordi, R., Memari, A.H., Mansournia, M.A., Jalali-Ghomi, M.: The effect of an ecological imagery program on soccer performance of elite players. Asian J. Sports Med. **3**(2) (2012). https://doi.org/10.5812/asjsm.34703

Influence of Delays in Functional Connectivity to Distinguish Motor Imagery Tasks

Pedro Felipe Giarusso de Vazquez[1,2] , Carlos Alberto Stefano Filho[1,2] ,
and Gabriela Castellano[1,2(✉)]

[1] Neurophysics Group, IFGW, UNICAMP, Campinas, Brazil
p263293@dac.unicamp.br, gabriela@ifi.unicamp.br
[2] BRAINN-FAPESP, Campinas, Brazil

Abstract. Motor imagery is a cognitive technique wherein individuals mentally rehearse bodily movements. Recognized for its alignment with various cognitive and motor functions, motor imagery has become pivotal in brain computer interface applications, especially for motor rehabilitation and neuroprosthetics. Using electroencephalography, a preferred modality for its portability and high temporal precision, our study sought to address the variability challenges in electroencephalography signals, often a bottleneck in brain computer interfaces efficacy. We delved into the role of delay occurrences in shaping the maximal functional connectivity within motor imagery electroencephalography tasks obtained with the motifs' synchronization method. Preliminary findings suggest that specific delay occurrences may play a crucial role in functional connectivity, holding implications for future brain computer interfaces applications and motor rehabilitation protocols.

Keywords: Brain-computer interfaces · Functional connectivity · Temporal delay analysis

1 Introduction

Motor Imagery (MI) is the cognitive ability to mentally rehearse bodily movements without any corresponding physical execution (Jeannerod, 2001). Such mental processes share parallels with a range of cognitive and motor behaviors, such as action observation, mental operations, and mental planning (Frank et al., 2001; Iacoboni et al., 1999). Given the specific brain patterns generated by this technique MI has emerged as a potent strategy for Brain Computer Interfaces (BCIs), especially in applications tailored for motor rehabilitation and neuroprosthetic interventions (Mcneill, n.d.; Padfield et al., 2019).

Among the tools to study brain activity, electroencephalography (EEG) stands out due to its portability, cost-effectiveness, and exceptional temporal resolution. However, one significant challenge within the BCI domain has been the inherent variability of EEG signals. Such variability often poses hurdles in achieving optimal performance, especially for functional BCIs. EEG-based MI-BCIs hold the potential to revolutionize

J. A. Riascos Salas et al. (Eds.): LAWCN 2023, CCIS 2108, pp. 118–127, 2024.
https://doi.org/10.1007/978-3-031-63848-0_9

motor rehabilitation, enhancing the efficacy of various traditional and innovative rehabilitation techniques. This includes physiotherapy and non-invasive brain stimulation
methods, synergizing with MI tasks to improve the overall quality and effectiveness
of motor recovery. A common approach in BCIs involves extracting the power spectral density (PSD) of the mu (μ) and beta (β) bands from the EEG signal and utilizing
them as features for classification (Li et al., 2015; Qin et al., 2010; Trad et al., 2011).
Alternatively, functional connectivity (FC) features have been leveraged to explore the
properties of brain networks in the context of BCI (Leeuwis et al., 2021). FC measures
the degree of similarity or synchronization between brain signals from distinct regions
and can be depicted as an adjacency matrix (for a comprehensive review on FC methods,
see (Bastos & Schoffelen, 2016)). Significantly, FC offers insights into the synchronous
activities across various brain areas, a dimension of information that mere PSD analysis
of the signal might overlook.

With the overarching goal to bolster the efficacy of MI-BCI classifications, our study
sets out to scrutinize the role of delay occurrences in establishing the maximal FC value,
computed using the motifs synchronization (MS) method (Rosário et al., 2015), within
MI-EEG tasks. It is important to stress that the original MS method of assessing FC uses
the maximum FC value among different delays between the series. These delays consider
that a signal might take a finite time to propagate from one brain region (one electrode) to
another. However, the central idea of our current research is rooted in the hypothesis that
longer latencies might prove to be more effective in discriminating between left-hand and
right-hand MI tasks, regardless of whether these latencies correspond to the maximum
connectivity values. Therefore, the principal objective of this study has been to investigate
this hypothesis, which we believe could offer new insights into the optimization of
MI-BCI systems.

2 Subjects, Materials and Methods

2.1 Subjects and Materials

Ten healthy volunteers (mean age 22 ± 3, 2 women), nine right-handed (with S9 being
left-handed) participated in 12 distinct MI-EEG sessions, recorded by a g.tec system
equipped with 16 dry electrodes and a sampling rate of 256 Hz. These sessions were
conducted on different days. Each individual session was structured into 5 runs, with
each run divided into task blocks (lasting 6 s), cue blocks (lasting 2 s), and rest blocks
(lasting 8 s).

The volunteers were seated comfortably in a relaxed position on a chair, with a
computer screen in front of them displaying the experimental protocol. Participants
were also asked to imagine the tactile sensation in their hands, enhancing the kinesthetic
experience to improve the MI experiment. The MI task required the participant to engage
in the mental simulation of opening and closing either their right (RH) or their left (LH)
hand. To ensure the participant's unpredictable response, tasks were randomized, yet
a consistent total of four tasks per hand was maintained in every run. The project was
approved by the local ethics committee (CAAE 58592916.9.1001.5404) and all subjects
signed an inform consent form, prior to data acquisition (Fig. 1).

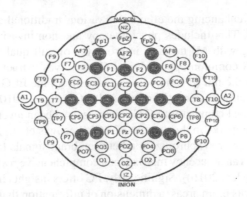

Fig. 1. Electrode positions used in this work (shown in red). (Color figure online)

Pre-processing of the EEG data was conducted using the EEGLAB software. This process involved several key steps. Initially, the first second of each run (rest block) was removed to eliminate the initial voltage spike. Subsequently, the signals were re-referenced to the common average reference (CAR) for enhanced signal stability. A high-pass filter with a cutoff frequency of 0.5 Hz was then applied to mitigate artifacts related to skin conductivity. Furthermore, independent component analysis (ICA) was employed to identify and remove eye blinking artifacts. This was achieved by comparing the ICA components with the signals from the AF3 and AF4 electrodes and analyzing the power spectra of these signals to accurately isolate and exclude the relevant artifacts.

For data processing, the EEG signals were band-pass filtered using EEGLAB's eegfilt function, which is a zero-phase filter. This was done to preserve the signal's frequency spectrum, specifically targeting the μ (8–12 Hz) and β (13–31 Hz) bands. One-second epochs were extracted for the analysis of functional connectivity, determined using the MS method [1], with time lags ranging from 0 to 8 samples (i.e., 0 to 31 ms) (Fig. 2).

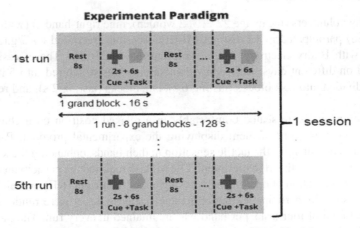

Fig. 2. MI sessions experimental paradigm. Each session was divided into five runs, and each run comprised alternating random blocks of left- or right-hand MI tasks, with rest blocks in-between.

2.2 Motifs Synchronization (MS) Functional Connectivity Method

EEG waveforms can be conceptualized as sequences composed of multiple patterns or points. The primary objective of the MS method is to quantify the synchronization degree between two EEG channels. This is achieved by counting the occurrences of specific patterns present between two time series (Rosário et al., 2015). In our study, we employed three-point motifs, which are showcased in Fig. 3.

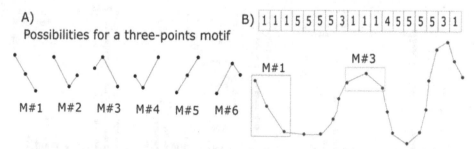

A)
Possibilities for a three-points motif

B) $\boxed{1\,1\,1\,5\,5\,5\,5\,3\,1\,1\,1\,4\,5\,5\,5\,5\,3\,1}$

M#1   M#2   M#3   M#4   M#5   M#6

M#1

M#3

Fig. 3. A) Three-point motifs patterns utilized in this study. B) Decomposition into 3-point patterns of a sample time series.

After converting the EEG time series into a series of motifs, they are pairwise compared, examining each point. This comparison can be performed considering various time lags between the series. In this study, we employed time lags, represented as τ, ranging from 0 to 8 points (these correspond to 0 to 31 ms, given the sampling rate of 256 Hz). Consequently, M_{xy} signifies the maximum number of instances where there's a correspondence between series x and y across different delay durations.

$$M_{xy} = \max\left(\sum_i^{L_m} J_i^{\tau_0}, \sum_i^{L_m} J_i^{\tau_1}, \ldots, \sum_i^{L_m} J_i^{\tau_n}\right) \tag{1}$$

with

$$J_i^\tau = \begin{cases} 1, & if x_{M_i} = y_{M_{i+\tau}} \\ 0, & otherwise \end{cases} \tag{2}$$

where x_{M_i} and y_{M_i} are the motif series, and L_m is the length of the motifs' series excluding the delays, which, for the 3-point motifs used here, is equal to $L - 2$, where L is the length of the EEG series. The synchronization coefficient is then given by:

$$Q_{xy} = \frac{\max(M_{xy}, M_{yx}) \cdot q_{xy}}{L_m} \tag{3}$$

where $q_{xy} = 1$ if $M_{xy} > M_{yx}$, otherwise $q_{xy} = -1$.

In words, if the motif count from x to y was greater than the count from y to x for varying delays, the former was deemed as a positive delay, while the latter was recognized as a negative delay. We restricted our analysis to the upper triangle of the delay matrix, leveraging the inherent symmetry of the connectivity matrix and, subsequently, the delay matrix.

3 Results

Focusing solely on the upper triangle of the delay matrix, Fig. 4 illustrates the frequency of each delay, i.e., the delay responsible for the highest degree of synchronization (i.e., maximal FC value), computed over all epochs, runs, sessions, and subjects, for each analyzed frequency band (μ and β).

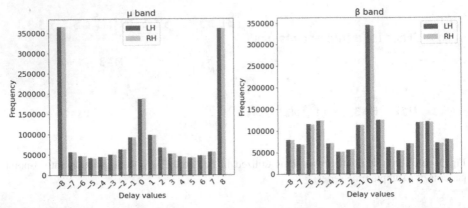

Fig. 4. Distribution of delay values that composed the maximum connectivity in μ (8-12Hz) and β (13-31Hz) bands.

In Table 1 (μ band) and Table 2 (β band), we have compiled the top 3 instances where the delay count differences between left-hand (LH) and right-hand (RH) tasks exceeded 100 for every second (1 to 6) of MI task. To aid in the interpretation of these results, values are color-coded for enhanced clarity: those highlighted in yellow signify the top three instances where the LH delay count was greater than the RH, and values highlighted in blue indicate the top three instances where the RH delay count exceeded that of the LH.

Table 1. Dominant differences in counts and correspondent LH–RH values for μ band. Here "second" refers to the 1s epochs within the 6s task block. An LH–RH negative value indicates that the RH count was higher than the LH count, and vice-versa.

Second	Delay value	LH–RH
1	8	139
	−8	−129
	5	−74
2	0	−165
	4	137
	−1	−84

(continued)

Table 1. (*continued*)

Second	Delay value	LH–RH
3	−1	−117
	−7	75
	5	61
4	3	−102
	−8	89
	−2	−87
5	2	86
	−8	84
	6	−61
6	−1	−125
	2	121
	0	104

Table 2. Dominant differences in counts and correspondent LH-RH values for β band. Here "second" refers to the 1s epochs within the 6s task block. An LH–RH negative value indicates that the RH count was higher than the LH count, and vice-versa.

Second	Delay value	LH-RH
1	−6	171
	0	−164
	5	−134
2	−5	162
	0	−156
	5	146
3	0	−111
	8	−105
	−7	98
4	−4	96
	8	89
	2	−72

(*continued*)

Table 2. (*continued*)

Second	Delay value	LH-RH
5	−6	158
	6	−134
	5	−104
6	3	87
	1	−86
	4	81

Figure 5 illustrates a comparison between delay occurrences to compose the maximal FC in left and right hemispheres in both μ and β bands.

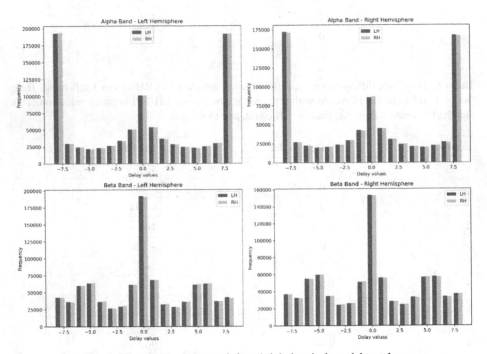

Fig. 5. Comparison between left and right hemisphere delay values

4 Discussion

The main aim of this work was to investigate the FC responses calculated from the motifs' method with different delays, and assess if these could bring a better separability between LH and RH tasks in the context of MI-BCIs.

In Fig. 4, we see that the μ band demonstrates a notable concentration on the 8-samples (~31 ms) delay chosen to contribute to maximum connectivity, while the β band has a similar concentration in the zero delay. MI activates the same neural circuits as voluntary movements, and the suppression of the μ-rhythm in EEG is a recognized marker of sensorimotor cortical activation during such imagery processes (Yakovlev et al., 2023). The β band power also decreases just before and during MI (Pfurtscheller & Neuper, 1997). Therefore, the consistent synchronization patterns observed, leading to the pronounced concentration on the 31 ms delay, could reflect the inherent neural consistency of MI tasks, especially given their tight link with actual motor processes. Conversely, the broader assortment of 'preferred' delays and the pronounced class discrepancy in the β band could be attributed to its multifaceted role in cognitive processing (Schmidt et al., 2019), possibly involving mechanisms beyond the straightforward motor neural circuits of the μ rhythm. Moreover, as Schmidt and colleagues suggests, the exact role of somatosensory afferentation in mental imagery processes remains ambiguous, which might account for the diversified and less predictable patterns seen in the β band.

Another interesting point, as aforementioned, is the fact that although more distributed, there is a peak on the zero delay for the β band. This is expected due to the volume conduction effect, which consists in that signals generated at a given cortex location may reach several (or all) electrode sites simultaneously due to the high conductivity properties of the tissues that lay between the cortex and the electrodes (Nunez et al., 1997)). Nevertheless, it is interesting to see that this peak did not happen for the μ band, as if this effect was somehow less pronounced for this band.

Regarding the discrimination between LH and RH, the diversification in delay choices, as seen in Table 1 and 2, offers insights into the intricacies of EEG synchronization during MI tasks. Four particular delays, zero and 8 samples (appearing twice), 5 (and −5) and 6 (and −6) (appearing 2 and 3 times, respectively), emerge as the most recurrent. This could suggest two primary modes of cortical communication during MI tasks: an immediate response (zero delay) reflecting the aforementioned volume conduction effect, and a slightly delayed response (8 samples) perhaps hinting at the involvement of other cognitive processes or feedback mechanisms in the sensorimotor network.

Interestingly, the μ band features just one highlighted value where RH > LH is the highest. This might indicate that somehow there is more than the volume conduction effect at play. Given the known suppression of the μ-rhythm during MI tasks, representing sensorimotor cortical activation, this may indicate that immediate activation patterns are more dominant in the right hemisphere for the specific task at hand.

Conversely, the β band, known for its broader role in cognitive and sensory processes, dominates the top values, which resonates with its multifunctionality. The variety of delay counts and the prominence of this band in the top values might reflect a combination of both motor and sensory processing, especially considering the still ambiguous role of somatosensory afferentation in MI. Such a dynamic might suggest that while the μ band is heavily associated with the fundamental motor imagery processes, the β band captures a richer tapestry of neural activities during MI, possibly indicating a blend of anticipation, feedback, and sensory integration.

Despite the above considerations, it is important to mention that none of the investigated delays resulted in a large count difference between LH and RH tasks. This can also be seen in Fig. 5, in which we separated the analysis by hemisphere – the counts among tasks remain similar for both hemispheres. If the maximum FC delays' distributions among tasks were different, we might be able to separate the tasks by computing FC for a chosen set of delays and attributing a given task to a larger connectivity at a given a delay. Therefore, as is, this approach did not seem to lead to the intended result.

It is also crucial to acknowledge the limitations of our approach. The study's scope was constrained by the number of subjects and the range of latencies examined. Future studies should aim to expand on these parameters to build a more comprehensive understanding of MI processes and their representation in EEG data.

5   Conclusion and Future Perspectives

In this study, we explored the impact of delay occurrences in shaping the maximal FC among MI-EEG tasks. We observed that certain delays played a pivotal role in creating an imbalance in occurrences between LH and RH tasks. Our primary hypothesis is that choosing delays always associated with the maximal FC, might not always be the most effective way in discriminating MI tasks. As a continuation of this work, the next step will be to delve into the FC features, derived from this method and using the delays highlighted in Tables 1 and 2 – with a special emphasis on the β band – for subsequent application in a classification model.

In conclusion, while our findings do offer new insights, they are not definitive. We advocate for these results to be viewed as a preliminary step towards a more nuanced understanding of MI and its neural underpinnings. We anticipate that subsequent research will build upon these foundations, providing greater clarity and confirming the trends suggested by our initial analyses.

Acknowledgements. This research was supported by Coordenação de Aperfeiçoamento de Pessoal de Nível Superior – Brazil (CAPES) – Grant 88887.910541/2023-00, Brazilian National Council for Scientific and Technological Development (CNPq) – Grant 304008/2021-4 and São Paulo Research Foundation – Grant 2013/07559-3.

References

Bastos, A.M., Schoffelen, J.M.: A tutorial review of functional connectivity analysis methods and their interpretational pitfalls. Front. Syst. Neurosci. **9**(JAN2016), 175 (2016). https://doi.org/10.3389/fnsys.2015.00175

Frank, M.J., Loughry, B., O'Reilly, R.C.: Interactions between frontal cortex and basal ganglia in working memory: a computational model. Cogn. Affect. Behav. Neurosci. **1**(2), 137–160 (2001). https://doi.org/10.3758/CABN.1.2.137

Iacoboni, M., Woods, R.P., Brass, M., Bekkering, H., Mazziotta, J.C., Rizzolatti, G.: Cortical mechanisms of human imitation. Science **286**(5449), 2526–2528 (1999). https://doi.org/10.1126/science.286.5449.2526

Jeannerod, M.: Neural simulation of action: a unifying mechanism for motor cognition. NeuroImage **14**(1 II), S103–S109 (2001). https://doi.org/10.1006/nimg.2001.0832

Leeuwis, N., Yoon, S., Alimardani, M.: Functional connectivity analysis in motor-imagery brain computer interfaces. Front. Hum. Neurosci. **15**, 732946 (2021). https://doi.org/10.3389/fnhum. 2021.732946

Li, M., Cui, Y., Hao, D., Yang, J.: An adaptive feature extraction method in BCI-based rehabilitation. J. Intell. Fuzzy Syst. **28**(2), 525–535 (2015). https://doi.org/10.3233/IFS-141329

Mcneill, M.E.: Mental Imagery and Its Potential for Physical Therapy (n.d.)

Nunez, P.L., et al.: EEG coherency I: statistics, reference electrode, volume conduction, Laplacians, cortical imaging, and interpretation at multiple scales. Electroencephalogr. Clin. Neurophysiol. **103**(5), 499–515 (1997). https://doi.org/10.1016/S0013-4694(97)00066-7

Padfield, N., Zabalza, J., Zhao, H., Masero, V., Ren, J.: EEG-based brain-computer interfaces using motor-imagery: techniques and challenges. Sensors **19**(6), 1423 (2019). https://doi.org/10.3390/s19061423

Pfurtscheller, G., Neuper, C.: Motor imagery activates primary sensorimotor area in humans. Neurosci. Lett. **239**(2–3), 65–68 (1997). https://doi.org/10.1016/S0304-3940(97)00889-6

Qin, Y., Xu, P., Yao, D.: A comparative study of different references for EEG default mode network: the use of the infinity reference. Clin. Neurophysiol. **121**(12), 1981–1991 (2010). https://doi.org/10.1016/j.clinph.2010.03.056

Rosário, R.S., Cardoso, P.T., Muñoz, M.A., Montoya, P., Miranda, J.G.V.: Motif-synchronization: a new method for analysis of dynamic brain networks with EEG. Physica A **439**, 7–19 (2015). https://doi.org/10.1016/j.physa.2015.07.018

Schmidt, R., Ruiz, M.H., Kilavik, B.E., Lundqvist, M., Starr, P.A., Aron, A.R.: Beta oscillations in working memory, executive control of movement and thought, and sensorimotor function. J. Neurosci. **39**(42), 8231–8238 (2019). https://doi.org/10.1523/JNEUROSCI.1163-19.2019

Trad, D., Al-Ani, T., Monacelli, E., Delaplace, S., Jemni, M.: Nonlinear and nonstationary framework for feature extraction and classification of motor imagery. In: IEEE International Conference on Rehabilitation Robotics (2011). https://doi.org/10.1109/ICORR.2011.5975488

Yakovlev, L., Syrov, N., Kaplan, A.: Investigating the influence of functional electrical stimulation on motor imagery related μ-rhythm suppression. Front. Neurosci. **17**, 1202951 (2023). https://doi.org/10.3389/fnins.2023.1202951

Impact of Ocular Artifact Removal on EEG-Based Color Classification for Locked-In Syndrome BCI Communication

Paal S. Urdahl, Vegard Omsland, Sandra Løkken, Mari Dokken,
Andres Soler(✉) ⓘ, and Marta Molinas ⓘ

Department of Engineering Cybernetics, Norwegian University of Science and
Technology, O.S. Bragstads Plass 2D, Trondheim 7034, Norway
{andres.f.soler.guevara,marta.molinas}@ntnu.no

Abstract. Locked-in Syndrome (LIS) is a neurological condition that results in paralysis of the body and the loss of communication abilities while leaving the patient's cognitive function unaffected [1]. This can significantly impact their quality of life, as previously simple tasks become impossible. Developing a communication system based on electroencephalogram (EEG) signals might, therefore, improve the quality of life of the affected. However, analyzing these signals can be challenging due to artifacts, especially ocular artifacts (OAs) from blinking [2]. This study investigates how four different OA removal techniques - Artifact Subspace Reconstruction (ASR), Independent Component Analysis (ICA), Signal-Space Projection (SSP), and a modified version of SSP - affect the accuracy of the convolutional neural networks (CNN) EEG-Net and EEGNeX in classifying RGB color exposure and color exposure against a rest-state. The results show that EEGNeX outperforms EEG-Net, improving classification by 4–9% depending on the OA removal technique used. While the OA removal techniques do not significantly differ, EEGNeX performs best with accuracies of over 71% for RGB classification and over 85% for Color/Rest classification. These results suggest that RGB color exposure elicits unique EEG patterns in the brain that could be used to develop a general communication model for LIS patients.

Keywords: Electroencephalography (EEG) · Locked-In Syndrome (LIS) · Brain-Computer Interface (BCI) · Color Classification · Convolutional Neural Network(CNN) · EEGNet · EEGNeX

1 Introduction

Electroencephalography (EEG) is a non-invasive measuring technique that involves placing electrodes on the scalp to measure the electrical signals of

P. S. Urdahl and V. Omsland—These authors contributed equally to this work.

J. A. Riascos Salas et al. (Eds.): LAWCN 2023, CCIS 2108, pp. 128–143, 2024.
https://doi.org/10.1007/978-3-031-63848-0_10

the brain. These signals exhibit varying statistical and frequency characteristics when an individual is exposed to different stimuli, making them a valuable tool for analysis and classification tasks. EEG signals are also utilized in developing Brain-Computer Interfaces (BCIs), which are computer applications that translate brain signals into outputs, often sensory or motor functions [3].

Locked-in Syndrome (LIS) is a rare neurological disorder caused by damage to the brainstem, leading to symptoms such as quadriplegia, loss of voluntary muscle control, and anarthria, also known as the inability to speak [1]. In the most common form of LIS, the affected only maintain control over vertical eye movement, which makes daily activities such as communicating and tending to basic needs incredibly challenging. However, in almost all cases of LIS, mental function remains fully intact. This is because the disorder originates in the brainstem, which is responsible for motor function, leaving the forebrain unaffected [4,5].

The unique circumstances of LIS patients present an opportunity for BCI systems to greatly improve their daily experience. Through analyzing and transforming the patient's EEG signals, these systems can generate motor responses or, as this study showcases, communication. Such advancements can significantly reduce the communication delay commonly experienced with traditional systems, ultimately leading to a higher quality of life for LIS patients [6]. Previous research [7–9] has revealed that EEG signal characteristics respond to RGB color exposure, making it possible to use machine learning techniques to develop a BCI system tailored to the specific needs of LIS patients. In such a system, the color classification would be the basis of what the patients are trying to communicate.

However, EEG signals may be susceptible to interference from unwanted signals, commonly referred to as artifacts. These artifacts can cause complications during the classification process, which in turn can lead to miscommunication and increased frustration for LIS patients. Notably, ocular artifacts (OAs) caused by blinking are particularly significant, as they can produce significant voltage fluctuations in the signals [10]. Therefore, this project has explored methods for both online and offline artifact removal and assessed their impact on RGB classification through the use of different neural network structures.

2 Methods

2.1 Dataset

The dataset was recorded at the NeuroImaging facilities of Aalto University in Helsinki [7]. The study focused on 31 subjects using a 64-channel cap from antNeuro, with a sampling rate of 1000 Hz. The electrodes were placed according to the international 10-10 system, as illustrated in Fig. 1. However, in this study, we utilize six channels for classification purposes: PO3, POz, PO4, O1, Oz, and O2. These channels were selected based on their location, as they are over the occipital lobe, which is responsible for visual input processing [2,10]. Unfortunately, some subjects did not perform well during the recording, either falling asleep or constantly moving, thus making their results unsuitable for analysis.

Also, some of the electrodes were not properly connected for some of the subjects when gathering data. Consequently, the analysis was conducted on only 22 out of the 31 subjects.

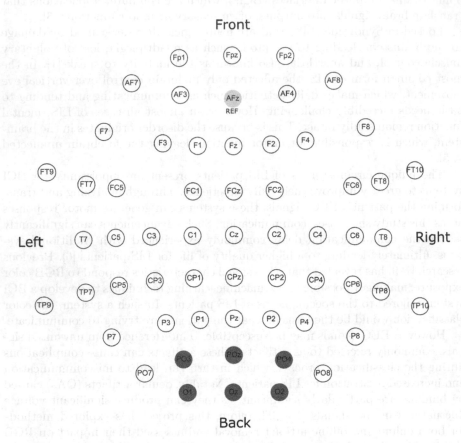

Fig. 1. Electrode placement for EEG signal acquisition using the 10–10 system. The electrodes in red indicate the channels used for classification.

2.2 Protocol and Data Collection

The experimental procedure, shown in Fig. 2, involved displaying a screen to the participants featuring a series of alternating colors, one of which was gray and contained a cross for resting their gaze. Each color was shown for 1.3 s, followed by the gray screen for a variable duration between 1.3 and 1.6 s to prevent the participants from becoming accustomed to the stimuli's timing. The order of the color presentation was randomized with the same purpose. The colors used were 0xFF0000 (Red), 0 × 008000 (Green), and 0 × 0000FF (Blue), and a total of 140 epochs of each color were recorded with four one-minute breaks interspersed throughout the recording. Participants were instructed not to blink during the color display, so it is expected that epochs containing OAs will be more prevalent during the gray screen [2].

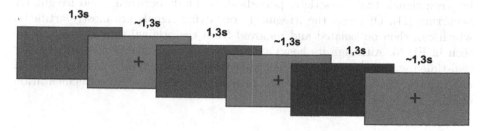

Fig. 2. Illustration describing how the data collection protocol was performed, reprinted from [2].

2.3 Data Preprocessing

Initially, the dataset was preprocessed by applying a notch filter near 50 Hz to eliminate powerline noise. Additionally, to narrow down the frequency range of interest and eliminate potential data acquisition noise, a bandpass filter between 0.1 Hz and 45 Hz was implemented. In pursuit of the objective of developing a real-time BCI, the signals were downsampled by a factor of 5, which effectively reduced the frequency to 200 Hz. This was a decision taken to avoid placing excessive computational demands on the equipment. A heavier computational load would have necessitated more processing power, resulting in equipment that is heavier and less portable. Additionally, not downsampling the signals would have resulted in longer time delays, an outcome that is undesirable when implementing a BCI.

2.4 Ocular Artifact Removal

The removal of the OAs has been achieved by utilizing four distinct artifact removal algorithms. These include Artifact Subspace Reconstruction (ASR), Independent Component Analysis (ICA), Signal-Space Projection (SSP), and a modified version of Signal-Space Projection (Modified SSP).

2.4.1   Independent Component Analysis

ICA is a widely used algorithm utilized to remove OAs. It separates components by the kurtosis of their amplitude distribution over time, thus distinguishing between signals that are strictly periodical, regularly occurring, and irregularly occurring [11]. Of these, the irregularly occurring signals are mostly artifacts, which can then be isolated and removed from the original signal. This can be seen in Fig. 3. Although its heavy computational load makes it unsuitable for real-time use, it remains a useful benchmark for comparing the other OA removal algorithms. The ICA algorithm used in this study is the *MNE*-implementation of ICA [12], based on [13–16].

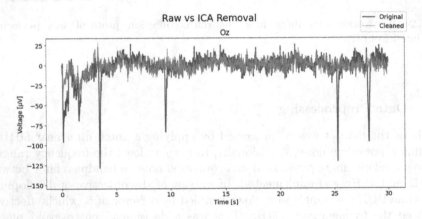

Fig. 3. Raw EEG signal plotted against the ICA cleaned EEG signal for channel Oz.

2.4.2   Artifact Subspace Reconstruction

The ASR technique is an algorithm that can remove offline artifacts from EEG data. By analyzing the statistical properties of the signal's covariance matrices through principal component analysis (PCA), the algorithm can detect irregularities and eliminate them. However, to achieve optimal results, the algorithm must first undergo a calibration phase using non-artifact contaminated data to learn the statistical properties of clean EEG data [17]. The implementation in this project is based on the ASR algorithm presented in [18], and an illustration of the OA removal can be seen in Fig. 4.

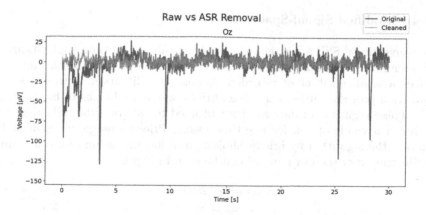

Fig. 4. Raw EEG signal plotted against the ASR cleaned EEG signal for channel Oz.

2.4.3   Signal-Space Projection

The technique of Signal-Space Projection (SSP) is widely employed in EEG to filter out unwanted noise from recorded signals. This involves projecting the signal onto a lower-dimensional subspace, which requires the average pattern across sensors while accounting for noise. This pattern is then utilized as a reference direction in sensor space, and the subspace is designed to be orthogonal to this noise direction [19]. Since the noise to be eliminated is OAs, the projection was computed using the electrooculogram (EOG) channels, resulting in a projection matrix that can be applied to the EEG data. By subtracting this projection from the data, the noise contributions from OAs are effectively removed, which can be seen in Fig. 5.

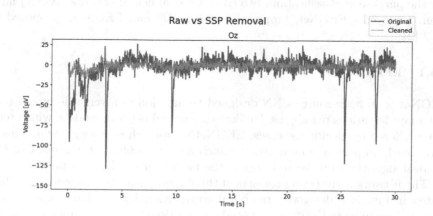

Fig. 5. Raw EEG signal plotted against the SSP cleaned EEG signal for channel Oz.

2.4.4   Modified Signal-Space Projection

The conventional SSP approach may not be ideal for real-time applications due to its lengthy calibration process. However, a modified version of this approach utilizes a smaller subset of recorded signals for calibration. During the data acquisition process, subjects are given brief one-minute breaks to blink as they wish. These segments of data are then utilized to calibrate the SSP algorithm, making it a viable option for real-time usage. Prior to usage, users must first calibrate the algorithm by briefly blinking and looking around for one minute. An illustration of the OA removal can be seen in Fig. 6.

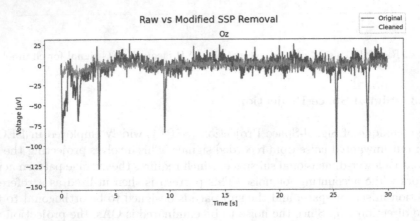

Fig. 6. Raw EEG signal plotted against the Modified SSP cleaned EEG signal for channel Oz.

2.5   Classification of EEG Data

For the purpose of classification, two convolutional neural networks (CNN) have been employed - EEGNet, proposed in 2018 [20], and EEGNeX, proposed in 2023 [21].

2.5.1   EEGNet

EEGNet is an open-source CNN designed to function as a versatile model that can adapt to various paradigms. Unlike other neural network models, which tend to be tailored to specific use cases, EEGNet's approach is more general. This is particularly important to our study, which aims to evaluate the impact of OA removal algorithms on the accuracy of the model across all subjects [2].

The network architecture consists of three fundamental components, as illustrated in Fig. 7: a depthwise temporal convolutional layer that helps extract temporal patterns in the data, a spatial convolutional layer that operates on the electrode axis, and a separable spatial convolution layer that reduces parameters and computational cost [20]. The exact implementation of the network is shown in Fig. 8.

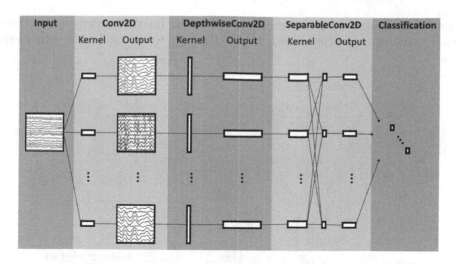

Fig. 7. A visualization of EEGNet, reprinted from [20].

Block	Layer	# filters	size	# params	Output	Activation	Options
1	Input				(C, T)		
	Reshape				(1, C, T)		
	Conv2D	F_1	(1, 64)	$64 * F_1$	(F_1, C, T)	Linear	mode = same
	BatchNorm			$2 * F_1$	(F_1, C, T)		
	DepthwiseConv2D	$D * F_1$	(C, 1)	$C * D * F_1$	$(D * F_1, 1, T)$	Linear	mode = valid, depth = D, max norm = 1
	BatchNorm			$2 * D * F_1$	$(D * F_1, 1, T)$		
	Activation				$(D * F_1, 1, T)$	ELU	
	AveragePool2D		(1, 4)		$(D * F_1, 1, T // 4)$		
	Dropout*				$(D * F_1, 1, T // 4)$		$p = 0.25$ or $p = 0.5$
2	SeparableConv2D	F_2	(1, 16)	$16 * D * F_1 + F_2 * (D * F_1)$	$(F_2, 1, T // 4)$	Linear	mode = same
	BatchNorm			$2 * F_2$	$(F_2, 1, T // 4)$		
	Activation				$(F_2, 1, T // 4)$	ELU	
	AveragePool2D		(1, 8)		$(F_2, 1, T // 32)$		
	Dropout*				$(F_2, 1, T // 32)$		$p = 0.25$ or $p = 0.5$
	Flatten				$(F_2 * (T // 32))$		
Classifier	Dense		$N * (F_2 * T // 32)$		N	Softmax	max norm = 0.25

Fig. 8. The network structure of EEGNet, reprinted from [20].

2.5.2 EEGNeX

EEGNeX serves as an open-source CNN that shares the same purpose as EEG-Net, which is to interpret mental constructs through EEG signals. This CNN was developed after evaluating 16 different neural network models in four BCI paradigms. The creators of EEGNeX assert that it outperforms existing methods, with classification accuracy increasing by up to 8.5% in different scenarios [21]. As such, it is worth examining how the classification accuracy varies when different OA removal algorithms are applied to the input signal.

While the network architecture of EEGNeX, shown in Fig. 9, is rooted in EEGNet, certain enhancements have been implemented to further elevate its performance. This includes fortifying the spatial representation extraction from the EEG data, substituting the separable representation with two 2D convolu tions in the general architecture, incorporating an inverse bottleneck structure, and expanding the receptive field of layers through dilation and fewer activations [21].

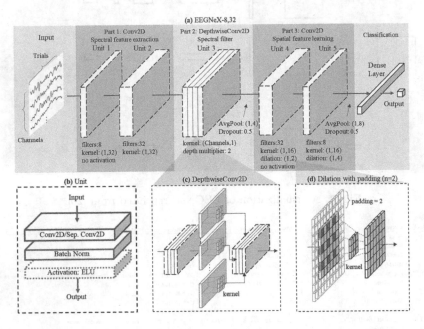

Fig. 9. The network structure of EEGNeX, reprinted from [21].

2.5.3 Training, Validation and Test Set

The data has been partitioned using a Leave-one-out Model (LOOM), which, in general, involves withholding a single data point during training to test the model's ability to generalize to unseen data. In this work, one subject was left out, while the remaining subjects were divided into an 80% training and 20% validation set. The model was then evaluated on the left-out subject to assess real-world performance. This process was repeated for each subject to assess the model's ability to generalize across all subjects.

2.6 Pipeline

The complete study pipeline can be seen in Fig. 10. The OA removal algorithms were used to process both the downsampled raw and filtered EEG data, which were then utilized to train the CNNs. Additionally, the neural networks were trained on both the raw and filtered data without undergoing OA removal.

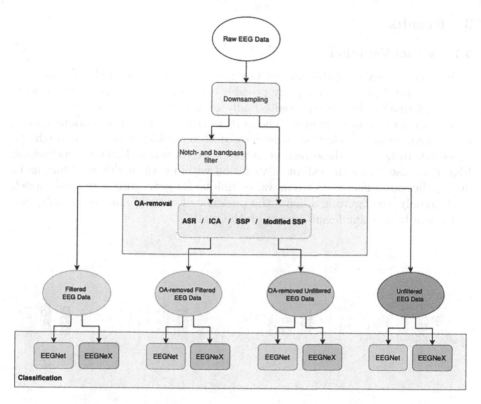

Fig. 10. Summary of the multiple processing pipelines. Here, unfiltered data is the same as raw data, meaning no band-pass or notch filter was applied.

2.7 Performance Metrics

In order to assess the effectiveness of the CNN models generated from the dataset variations, we will be utilizing the accuracy statistic. This statistic is defined as:

$$Accuracy = \frac{TP + TN}{TP + TN + FP + FN} \qquad (1)$$

where TP represents the number of true positives, TN represents the number of true negatives, FP represents the number of false positives, and FN represents the number of false negatives. The optimal value for accuracy is 1 or 100%, which would indicate that all predictions were correct.

3   Results

3.1   Model Variation

In Fig. 11, a display of the various OA removal methods and their respective outcomes are shown, including any possible outliers. These outliers are subjects that performed either unexpectedly badly or unexpectedly well, therefore not representing the general models. The outliers can originate from various places, i.e. anomalous data collection or inter-subject variability, meaning it might be necessary to not give these results as much weight when drawing conclusions. Figure 11 also shows the extent of variation within each model, enabling us to decide the most effective OA removal technique for generating a general model. Additionally, the figure highlights the presence of outliers among the subjects, which can have a significant impact on the model.

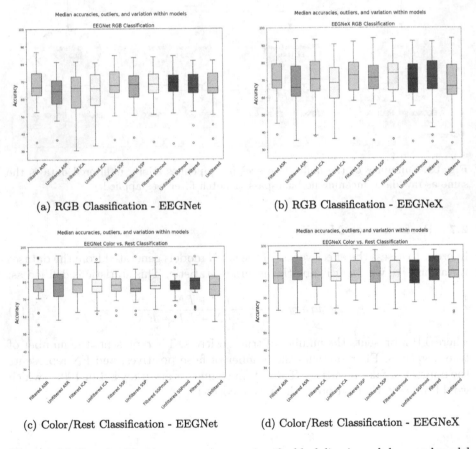

(a) RGB Classification - EEGNet   (b) RGB Classification - EEGNeX

(c) Color/Rest Classification - EEGNet   (d) Color/Rest Classification - EEGNeX

Fig. 11. Median classification accuracy, meaning the black line in each box, and model variation for all pipelines (Color figure online).

3.2   RGB Classification

Table 1 displays the accuracy outcomes for the classification of RGB colors. The table showcases the classification results for the various OA removal algorithms for both filtered and unfiltered input signals. Across all OA removal algorithms, there was an improvement in accuracy when EEGNeX was used. This improvement varies between 3% and 5% based on the OA removal technique. For the models trained on filtered data, Modified SSP performed the best. For unfiltered data, SSP performed the best. In general, the accuracies also decrease somewhat when using unfiltered compared to filtered data. In addition to this, the outlier corrected results are shown, which is the mean accuracies when the outliers depicted in Fig. 11 are omitted. These results show an increase in accuracy of around 2%, as the RGB models only produce outliers with very low performance. Again, Modified SSP performs the best for filtered data, while normal SSP performs the best for unfiltered data.

Table 1. Mean Accuracies for EEGNet and EEGNeX for RGB Classification. *OC - Outlier Corrected.*

	OA Correction	EEGNet	EEGNeX	OC EEGNet	OC EEGNeX
Filtered	ASR	66.7%	70.2%	68.2%	71.7%
	ICA	63.0%	69.9%	63.0%	71.4%
	SSP	67.1%	71.0%	68.5%	72.7%
	Modified SSP	66.7%	**71.1%**	68.2%	**72.8%**
	No OA Correction	65.6%	68.6%	68.2%	71.9%
Unfiltered	ASR	63.6%	67.9%	64.9%	67.9%
	ICA	64.0%	66.6%	66.5%	66.6%
	SSP	65.9%	**70.0%**	67.2%	**71.7%**
	Modified SSP	66.7%	69.8%	68.3%	71.5%
	No OA Correction	65.8%	67.5%	68.3%	69.1%

3.3   Color/Rest Classification

Table 2 displays the accuracy results for the classification of RGB versus gray as illustrated in **Fig.** 2. Generally, the accuracies are noticeably higher than those for RGB Classification, which is expected given that there are only two targets to classify instead of three. Notably, the filtered data showed an increase in accuracy of 4%-6% between EEGNet and EEGNeX, while the unfiltered data showed an increase of 7–8%. Optimal results were obtained when using no OA removal on filtered data or ASR on unfiltered data. Outlier correction shows that using no OA removal resulted in the best accuracy outcomes for both filtered and unfiltered data.

4   Discussion

The primary objective of this research is to explore the impact of OA removal algorithms on the classification accuracy between EEGNet and EEGNeX, with the ultimate goal of developing a functional and reliable BCI communication system for individuals with Locked-In Syndrome.

Table 2. Mean Accuracies for EEGNet and EEGNeX for Color/Rest Classification. *OC - Outlier Corrected.*

	OA Correction	EEGNet	EEGNeX	OC EEGNet	OC EEGNeX
Filtered	ASR	78.3%	83.7%	79.7%	83.7%
	ICA	76.7%	83.1%	76.8%	83.1%
	SSP	77.5%	84.1%	78.2%	84.1%
	Modified SSP	78.3%	84.4%	78.3%	84.4%
	No OA Correction	78.8%	**85.1%**	81.1%	**85.1%**
Unfiltered	ASR	77.5%	**84.6%**	77.5%	84.6%
	ICA	76.9%	84.1%	76.9%	84.1%
	SSP	76.9%	83.8%	77.6%	83.8%
	Modified SSP	76.8%	84.0%	77.9%	84.0%
	No OA Correction	76.8%	84.2%	76.8%	**86.5%**

The findings of this research demonstrate that EEGNeX consistently outperforms EEGNet in both RGB classification and Color/Rest classification. This suggests that EEGNeX may have better adaptability for extracting features from EEG signals relevant to color classification. These results are in line with the findings in [21], showing that EEGNeX outperforms existing methods.

One notable observation is the absence of a significant difference between the OA removal methods. This implies that both EEGNet and EEGNeX are effective in mitigating the influence of OAs.

In the rest periods, the subjects were instructed to blink freely, which raises an intriguing consideration. The presence of blinks during rest periods introduces the possibility that the neural networks could be performing classification based on the presence of blinks rather than the underlying EEG signal. Interestingly, it was observed that the classification accuracy of Color/Rest on the OA-cleaned signals performed comparably to the signals where OAs were present. This finding highlights the robustness of the neural network in distinguishing rest periods. While the presence of OAs may raise questions about the network's decision-making process during rest periods, the equivalent performance of OA-cleaned signals and signals with OAs suggests that the network effectively leverages the underlying EEG features.

In contrast, during the RGB classification, subjects were explicitly instructed not to blink. This results in EEG signals with significantly fewer blinks compared to the rest periods. The reduced presence of blinks during RGB classification indicates that the neural network relies on the EEG features associated with color stimuli to make accurate classifications.

One important finding in this study is that the most substantial increase in model accuracy arises from changes in the neural network rather than variations in OA removal methods. This finding emphasizes the important role of the neural network structure in EEG-based color classification tasks. It will be important in this field to prioritize the selection and optimization of neural network architecture when designing experiments.

An observation in this study is that EEGNet appears to produce more outliers in the Color/Rest classification compared to EEGNeX, as shown in Fig. 11. Interestingly, this is not as pronounced in the RGB classification, where both networks exhibit a similar number of outliers. This higher incidence of outliers for EEGNet might suggest that this network architecture does not generalize as well in this specific scenario. Moreover, when considering the variation in the models, it appears quite similar across the neural network architectures. While it is difficult to determine whether this uniformity makes the model more or less general, it is noteworthy that EEGNeX produces fewer outliers. This may indicate a favorable aspect of their performance, as fewer outliers may enhance the overall robustness and reliability of the model's predictions.

While the results indicate that the general model performs well in color classification, the persistence of outliers is a noteworthy issue. This outcome is likely attributed to the inherent variations in individuals' responses to color stimuli. Such individual differences have been observed in previous EEG studies, in particular when creating individual subject models for RGB classification [7,22]. The difference in performance is noticeable across participants due to the individual differences. In this study, individual models were not evaluated, but this will be explored in future work.

While not tested in this study, modifications to the ASR algorithm have led to the development of Riemannian Artifact Subspace Reconstruction (rASR), which calculates a robust estimate of the covariance matrix for the entire dataset instead of individual matrices for each time period. This significantly reduces computational load, allowing for real-time implementation of the algorithm for online artifact correction [23]. According to [23], this version of the algorithm outperforms the one used in this work, and considering ASR performs well in this work, it is therefore interesting to investigate rASR for future work.

5 Conclusion

This study demonstrates the possibility of distinguishing EEG signals elicited by RGB colors through general neural network models. The findings suggest that EEGNeX is superior in extracting signal information, resulting in classification accuracy of up to 85% for the case of Color/Rest classification and 71% for RGB classification. This implies that generalized models can be applied to this task, reducing the need for individual-specific models that can be time-consuming and expensive to develop. Nonetheless, further enhancements are necessary to create a dependable and user-friendly communication system for LIS patients since an accuracy rate of 71% is inadequate for error-free communication. The results also show that the removal of ocular artifacts from blinking does not affect classification accuracy drastically. This could argue that online removal of ocular artifacts might not be necessary, as EEGNeX extracts information well, even from raw unfiltered EEG data. However, this does need more investigation, as experiments conducted closer to real-life scenarios might show that EEG artifacts more strongly affect the classification of the general models. Nevertheless, the outcomes are encouraging, and the use of EEGNeX suggests that advancements are being made, indicating that a BCI communication system for LIS communication is not far away.

References

1. Schnakers, C., et al.: Cognitive function in the locked-in syndrome. J. Neurol. **255**, 323–330 (2008). https://doi.org/10.1007/S00415-008-0544-0/METRICS
2. Løkken, S.G., Dokken, M.H.: Automated Detection and Removal of EEG Artifacts for an RGB Stimulation-Based Brain-Computer Interface. Masters thesis, Norwegian University of Science and Technology, Trondheim, Norway (2023). https://hdl.handle.net/11250/3096563
3. Siuly, S., Li, Y., Zhang, Y.: EEG Signal Analysis and Classification. Springer, Cham, Switzerland (2016). https://doi.org/10.1007/978-3-319-47653-7
4. Das, J.M., Anosike, K., Asuncion, R.M.D.: Locked-in syndrome. Encyc. Neurol. Sci. 916 (2023). https://doi.org/10.1016/B978-0-12-385157-4.00334-1
5. Markand, O.N.: Electroencephalogram in "locked-in" syndrome. Electroencephalography Clin. Neurophysiol. **40**, 529–534 (1976). https://doi.org/10.1016/0013-4694(76)90083-3
6. Johansson, V., Soekadar, S.R., Clausen, J.: Locked out: Ignorance and responsibility in brain-computer interface communication in locked-in syndrome. Cambridge Quart. Healthcare Ethics **26**, 555–576 (2017). https://doi.org/10.1017/S0963180117000081
7. Ludvigsen, S.L., Buøen, E.H., Soler, A.,Molinas, M.: Searching for unique neural descriptors of primary colours in EEG signals: A classification study. Lecture Notes in Computer Science (including subseries Lecture Notes in Artificial Intelligence and Lecture Notes in Bioinformatics) 12960 LNAI, 277–286 (2021) https://doi.org/10.1007/978-3-030-86993-9_26/FIGURES/2
8. Wu, Y., Mao, Y., Feng, K., Wei, D., Song, L.: Decoding of the neural representation of the visual RGB color model. PeerJ Comput. Sci. **9**, 1376 (2023). https://doi.org/10.7717/PEERJ-CS.1376/SUPP-5
9. Torres-Garcia, A.A., Moctezuma, L.A., Asly, S., Molinas, M.: Discriminating between color exposure and idle state using EEG signals for BCI application. In: 2019 7th E-Health and Bioengineering Conference, EHB 2019 (2019). https://doi.org/10.1109/EHB47216.2019.8969919
10. Riitta Hari, P.D., Aina Puce, P.: MEG-EEG Primer. Oxford University Press,Oxford, UK (2017). https://doi.org/10.1093/med/9780190497774.001.0001

11. Vigirio, R.: Extraction of ocular artefacts from EEG using independent component analysis. Electroencephalogr. Clin. Neurophysiol. **103**, 395–404 (1997)
12. MNE-python :mne.preprocessing.ICA – MNE 1.5.1 documentation. Accessed Sep 2023. https://mne.tools/stable/generated/mne.preprocessing.ICA.html (2023)
13. Hyvärinen, A.: Fast and robust fixed-point algorithms for independent component analysis. IEEE Trans. Neural Netw. **10**, 626–634 (1999). https://doi.org/10.1109/72.761722
14. Bell, A.J., Sejnowski, T.J.: An information-maximization approach to blind separation and blind deconvolution. Neural Comput. **7**, 1129–1159 (1995). https://doi.org/10.1162/NECO.1995.7.6.1129
15. Lee, T.W., Girolami, M., Sejnowski, T.J.: Independent component analysis using an extended infomax algorithm for mixed subgaussian and supergaussian sources. Neural Comput. **11**, 417–441 (1999). https://doi.org/10.1162/089976699300016719
16. Ablin, P., Cardoso, J.F., Gramfort, A.: Faster independent component analysis by preconditioning with hessian approximations. IEEE Trans. Signal Process. **66**, 4040–4049 (2018). https://doi.org/10.1109/TSP.2018.2844203
17. Chang, C.Y., Hsu, S.H., Pion-Tonachini, L., Jung, T.P.: Evaluation of artifact subspace reconstruction for automatic artifact components removal in multi-channel EEG recordings. IEEE Trans. Biomed. Eng. **67**, 1114–1121 (2020). https://doi.org/10.1109/TBME.2019.2930186
18. Mullen, T.R., et al.: Cauwenberghs, G.:Real-time neuroimaging and cognitive monitoring using wearable dry EEG. IEEE Trans. Bio-medical Eng. **62**, 2553–2567 (2015). https://doi.org/10.1109/TBME.2015.2481482
19. Tesche, C.D., Uusitalo, M.A., Ilmoniemi, R.J., Huotilainen, M., Kajola, M., Salonen, O.: Signal-space projections of meg data characterize both distributed and well-localized neuronal sources. Electroencephalograph. Clin. Neurophysiol. **95**, 189–200 (1995). https://doi.org/10.1016/0013-4694(95)00064-6
20. Lawhern, V.J., Solon, A.J., Waytowich, N.R., Gordon, S.M., Hung, C.P., Lance, B.J.: Eegnet: a compact convolutional neural network for EEG-based brain-computer interfaces. J. Neural Eng. **15**, 056013 (2018). https://doi.org/10.1088/1741-2552/AACE8C
21. Chen, X., Teng, X., Chen, H., Pan, Y., Geyer, P.: Toward reliable signals decoding for electroencephalogram: a benchmark study to eegnex. Biomed. Signal Process. Contr. **87**, 1746–8094 (2024). https://doi.org/10.1016/j.bspc.2023.105475
22. Fløtaker, S., Soler, A., Molinas, M.: Discriminating between color exposure and idle state using EEG signals for BCI application. In: 45th Annual International Conference of the IEEE Engineering in Medicine and Biology Society EMBC (2023)
23. Blum, S., Jacobsen, N.S.J., Bleichner, M.G., Debener, S.: A riemannian modification of artifact subspace reconstruction for EEG artifact handling. Front. Human Neurosci. **13**, 421678 (2019). https://doi.org/10.3389/FNHUM.2019.00141/BIBTEX

Author Index

A
Appriou, Aurélien 25
Avilez, Karla 43

B
Bastos-Filho, Teodiano 3
Bessa, Wallace Moreira 57
Blanco-Diaz, Cristian Felipe 3

C
Castellano, Gabriela 118
Cota, Vinícius Rosa 57

D
da Silva Lima, Gabriel 57
de Vazquez, Pedro Felipe Giarusso 118
Delisle-Rodriguez, Denis 3
Dokken, Mari 128

F
Filho, Carlos Alberto Stefano 118

G
Gonzalez-Cely, Aura Ximena 3
Guerrero-Mendez, Cristian David 3
Guzmán Riaño, Lina María Estefanía 106

H
Hernández, José Armando 14
Hernández-Riveros, Jesús-Antonio 69

J
Jaramillo-Isaza, Sebastián 3

L
Løkken, Sandra 128
Lotte, Fabien 25

M
Mancera Soto, Erica Mabel 106
Molinas, Marta 128
Müller, Oliver 95

O
Omsland, Vegard 128
Orjuela-Cañon, Alvaro David 95

P
Pineda Ortiz, Gustavo Adolfo 106

R
Rico-Mesa, Edgar-Mario 69
Ruiz-Olaya, Andrés Felipe 3

S
Soler, Andres 128

T
Torres-Narváez, Martha-Rocio 95

U
Urdahl, Paal S. 128

V
Villota, Hernán 43

© The Editor(s) (if applicable) and The Author(s), under exclusive license
to Springer Nature Switzerland AG 2024
J. A. Riascos Salas et al. (Eds.): LAWCN 2023, CCIS 2108, p. 145, 2024.
https://doi.org/10.1007/978-3-031-63848-0

Printed in the United States
by Baker & Taylor Publisher Services

Printed in the United States
by Baker & Taylor Publisher Services